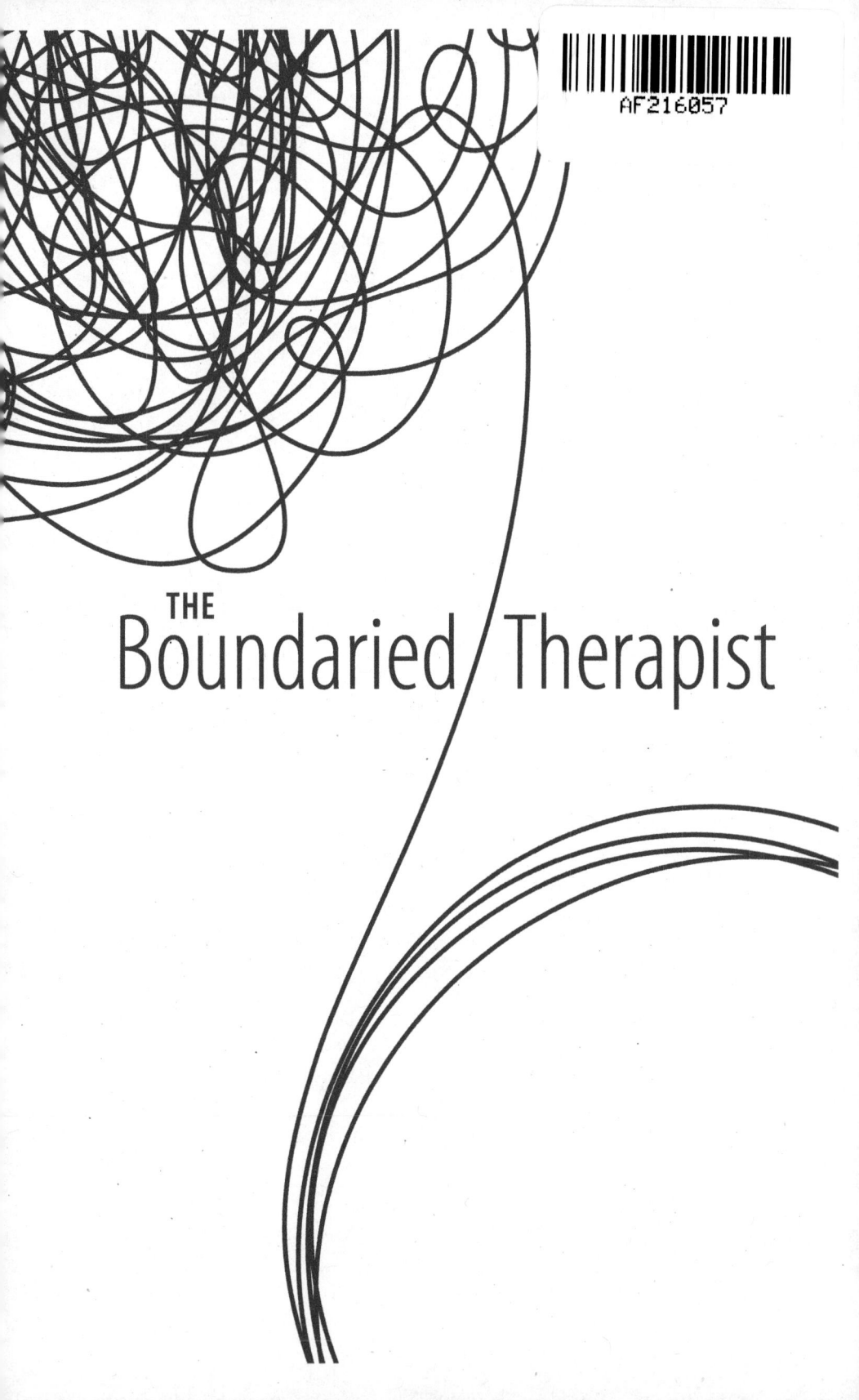

THE
Boundaried Therapist

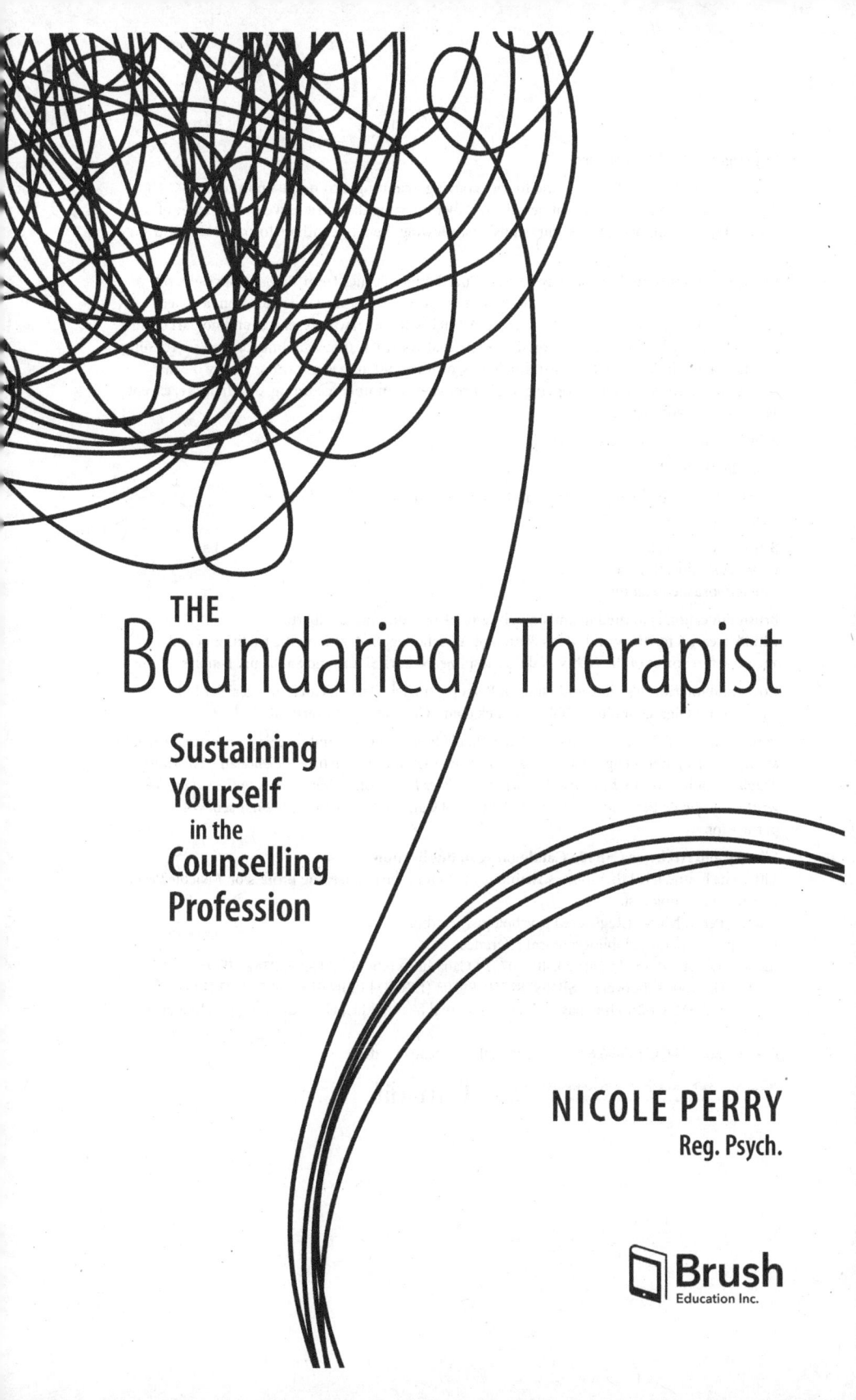

THE
Boundaried Therapist

**Sustaining
Yourself**
in the
**Counselling
Profession**

NICOLE PERRY
Reg. Psych.

Brush
Education Inc.

Printed and manufactured in Canada

24 25 26 27 28 5 4 3 2 1

This book is available in print, PDF, and Global Certified Acessible™ EPUB formats.

Brush Education Inc.
www.brusheducation.ca
contact@brusheducation.ca

Brush Education is located in amiskwaciwâskahikan, Edmonton, Alberta, within Treaty 6 territory and Métis Nation of Alberta Region 4, and on the traditional and ancestral territories of the Nêhiyawak, Denesuliné, Nakota Sioux, and Saulteaux Peoples.

Cover and interior design: Carol Dragich Bishop, Dragich Design; Cover images: Scribble — iStock.com / Olga Ubirailo. Bubbles – iStock.com / Chainarong Prasertthai

Parts of this book have been adapted from Nicole Perry's courses and teaching resources available at http://www.embodiedpsychology.ca/, and from the *Intimate Partner Violence* and *Vicarious Trauma* volumes of the *Inclusive Practices Guidelines for Assisting Newcomers to Canada* series, written by Nicole Perry for the United Cultures of Canada Association (2020), used with permission.

Library and Archives Canada Cataloguing in Publication
Title: The boundaried therapist : sustaining yourself in the counselling profession / Nicole Perry, registered psychologist.
Names: Perry, Nicole (Registered psychologist), author.
Description: Includes bibliographical references.
Identifiers: Canadiana (print) 20240350731 | Canadiana (ebook) 20240350782 | ISBN 9781550599480 (softcover) | ISBN 9781550599503 (EPUB) | ISBN 9781550599497 (PDF)
Subjects: LCSH: Counseling psychologists—Mental health. | LCSH: Counseling psychologists—Job stress.
Classification: LCC BF636.64 .P47 2024 | DDC 158.3023—dc23

We acknowledge the support of the Government of Canada
Nous reconnaissons l'appui du gouvernement du Canada | Canadä

For my parents.

Table of Contents

Acknowledgments

I would like to thank everyone who shared their experiences with me about boundaries, including Thomas Benowicz, Melody Cesar, Laura Kennedy, Susan Larcombe, Sophia Parks, Claire Wilde, Jason Wu, Sholly Scarlet, and Olga Yakovlyeva. I also want to thank all the early readers who had their eyes on my work before it was ever picked up by an editor: Marc Colbourne, Maija Prakash, Stephanie Hawryliw, and Julie Johnston. And of course, thank you to Brush Education and my editor, Kay Rollans, for reaching out to me with what was essentially a cold call—proving that seeds planted can and do grow in time. Finally, thank you to my own therapists and the peer groups that have sustained and supported me over time.

Introduction

I've been working in the helping profession since I was eighteen years old. For most of my young life, I took pride in doing hard things: I was successful in school, receiving awards and scholarships for academic achievements. I was a high-performing athlete on one of the best cheer teams in the country. In my professional life, I worked nights, I did shift work, I sometimes held several jobs at once, and I often took hard cases with little to no support. It felt good to be able to push the limits of my mind and body and to see what I was capable of.

I've also dealt with migraine disease since I was a teenager. At first, attacks were few and far between, and could usually be dealt with by going into a dark room and taking over-the-counter pain relievers. Then, as an adult still in the early stages of my career as a psychologist, my body finally said stop. The chronic stress I'd been dealing with over the years, combined with the acute stress of a particularly challenging work situation, was too much for my body to handle. I began having more and more migraine attacks. It progressed to a point where I was dealing with high-intensity pain daily.

While all of this was happening, I was also beginning a relationship with someone new, my now husband. The pain I was in dominated the early days of our relationship. My most vivid memories of that time are of my husband sitting beside me as I cried in the bathtub, or holding me while I lay in a basement room, unable to string together more than a few words. He whispered to me, telling me stories in the most soothing voice he could muster until, at last, my body let me sleep.

Some mornings I'd wake up and just be grateful to be free of the pain for a little while. Other times I'd feel the pressure of pain-free time like a weight on my chest. I knew I only had so much of it before the pain would return. Intense migraines loomed over me in this way for more than a year. My time and energy were consumed by simply trying to manage them, and it wasn't long before despair and hopelessness started to flood in.

My mind wanted to keep going, but my body absolutely couldn't. When I kept pushing, ignoring my body's signals, my body pushed back—hard.

As a result, I had to reckon with what I was truly capable of, which at the time wasn't more than a few hours of work each day. I had to be willing to cancel a day of work when pain started to set in, and I had to start setting boundaries around the hours that I was in the office.

Fast forward a decade or so and my health is much better, but I know that I will never be able—or willing—to take on as much as I used to. I know my body will never be the same from the experiences I've gone through. It's not capable of withstanding as much as it once was, and it's constantly reminding me of that in new and interesting ways. I have no doubt that the chronic pain I live with now is at least partially linked to my experience of being pushed, and pushing myself, too far.

Chronic pain has taught me humility. When I first started struggling with pain, I was caught up in a shame-fuelled belief system that I wasn't even aware of. My young brain believed that if something was difficult, you just had to try harder. The pain that started taking over my life was difficult, but I stubbornly thought I could beat it just by trying harder—that I *should* be able to work a certain number of hours a week, that I *should* be able to go to social events without it triggering pain, and that I *could* do this if I tried in the right way. Of course I thought this way; my experience supported it, and so did every institution I'd been a part of to that point.

I'd also been taught that being a team player meant showing up to every practice (or event, or meeting, or appointment) and giving 110 percent, no matter how I was feeling or what was going on for me. With my cheerleading team, I remember practising and performing through injuries that should have taken weeks to heal but, because I kept re-injuring them, took months. I remember the pressure of delivering perfect performances because making a mistake meant you might be cut from a routine rather than supported to learn and improve.

My early lessons about how to "succeed"—working as hard as possible, giving it everything every time, striving for perfection, and never making a mistake—didn't translate well into my work as a therapist. There, I couldn't be "perfect"; the issues that I was facing, that I was helping my clients through, were beyond my capacity to fix. I ran into structural issues that could never be resolved by one person, no matter how idealistic, bright eyed, and bushy tailed. I encountered the limits of my own skill and understanding, but I didn't have any practice with this way of being—so when I couldn't figure out how to help a client or had to say no to a request, I panicked. According to everything I had learned, disappointing someone, whether it be a teammate, an employer, or a client, was the worst thing I could do and I always felt on the edge of doing so.

I know I'm not alone in this. In my work consulting with and supervising other therapists, I have fielded many boundary-related questions, from "How many clients should I see per week?" to "What's a reasonable cancellation policy?" Underneath these specific questions, I find therapists are eager to understand something deeper: How do I work in a way that's sustainable for me? How do I continue to open my heart without going under? How do I deal with the guilt when I need to say no? The more I talk with clients, colleagues, and supervisees, the clearer it is that listening and responding to our needs is hard for almost everyone. Most therapists I've encountered struggle to do in our own lives what we try to help others do in theirs: set and maintain boundaries that nurture and sustain us. From the start of our training, we are taught to think about client needs, but it is much less common to be taught to think about our own. We are (necessarily) made aware of practical and financial barriers for clients and encouraged to reduce these barriers as much as possible. There is no arguing that conversations around client needs are important, but the conversation around our own emotional, practical, and financial needs as therapists is conspicuously missing.

As therapists, we often choose our working hours and location based on what would be convenient for clients, without considering what would work for ourselves and our own lives. We offer reduced rates because clients are financially struggling without looking at our own budget and financial needs. We take on clients because we see their need for services without getting clear on whether we are the best fit for their presenting issues, and whether we truly have capacity within our caseload. We take on workplace contracts that meet the needs of an employer without really questioning whether they meet our own.

This happens in part because we don't know our boundaries and needs until we've had a chance to do some reality testing. But I think there are other reasons that boundary-setting as a therapist is especially difficult. For one, we therapists are human. All the barriers and challenges of life—from societal expectations to structural inequities to personal experiences—affect us as much as they affect anyone else. Additionally, we work in a profession that requires us to be able to access deep empathy and compassion on a daily basis. When you're that tuned in to other people's pain, the idea of adding to it—by having to cancel an appointment, for example—can be daunting. It can be hard to imagine disappointing those who have already been so let down by the people and systems that should have been there to support them. Consequently, many of us tend toward what feels easier in the moment: overextending ourselves so that others can flourish.

While there's more in the zeitgeist in recent years on the importance of boundary-setting and tips on how to set them, I find deep understanding around what boundaries actually are to be generally lacking. My own clinical and supervisory experience has demonstrated the importance of boundary-setting practices to the sustainability and fulfilment of therapists and other counselling professionals, yet this is rarely a topic that is explored in depth in therapist education or professional development. I was lucky to learn about boundaries very early on in my career, while working on a local suicide distress line. These early lessons were about teaching clients how to have good boundaries, and they have been invaluable to my career. But looking back on them now, I notice that they had nothing to do with my own capacity or well-being. I never thought, back then, about how they might apply to my own life as a therapist.

Education and resources that do address boundaries for therapists tend to specifically address professional boundaries—that is, boundaries focused almost entirely on appropriate relationships with clients, and those specifically defined by professional licensing and regulatory bodies. It is absolutely vital to understand the limits of client–therapist interactions, and maintaining these boundaries is crucial to both ethical practice and our professional standing as licensed therapists. But professional boundaries aren't enough to address the therapist in a wholistic way. They don't contemplate the many other aspects of counselling work to which boundary-setting may apply in equally important ways—around the time we give to it, for example, or the emotional investment we are able to make. This educational lacuna is reflected in the research: as one study notes, very little attention has been paid to the issue of work–life balance for psychologists outside the academic setting, or for graduate and practicum students.[1]

In the absence of comprehensive education on the topic, misconceptions about boundaries fill the void. In particular, we're often led to believe that personal boundaries and interpersonal connection are at odds with one another. The truth is that boundaries *allow* for openness. We cannot connect with others when we are not connected with ourselves—it just isn't possible. Boundaries help us remain connected with ourselves, and thus with our clients, by protecting us from burnout, vicarious trauma, and resentment. We're also often taught, implicitly or explicitly, to avoid disappointing others, especially our clients, and that boundaries can be catalysts of disappointment. It is true that setting a boundary might disappoint a client but, in reality, our professional and personal capacity has real limits that can't be avoided. This means that disappointing our clients is an inevitable part of the work, no matter how much we try to avoid it. It is important to remember that our job is not to categorically avoid disappointing clients (or colleagues, or employers); our job is to remain kind and connected when disappointment happens. This is where boundaries play an integral role. Boundaries are not about controlling our clients' reactions to difficult news or their behaviour toward us, but about honouring our own needs and limits in ways that allow us to show up not only for ourselves, but for others.

When I teach about boundaries, I often notice that students and participants come in with the idea that boundaries are nice for those who can afford them, but definitely a luxury. There's also a sentiment that therapist boundaries are okay in certain low-stakes situations, but not once things get serious—not once we're dealing with "real" issues like interpersonal violence, suicide, and homelessness, for example. I've spoken with some supervisees who have been genuinely worried that if they don't respond with everything they have and more in these types of life-or-death situations, they will be responsible for any harm that comes to their client.

What I've gleaned in my years of learning from, working with, and speaking to clients, colleagues, and supervisees is that boundaries are absolutely *not* just for the privileged folks out there or the trivial matters in our lives. Boundaries are important in all our day-to-day interactions, and they become downright necessary when those day-to-day interactions involve responding to crises and difficult situations in others' lives.

Most of us *can* fit in an extra hour of work when there's a client emergency, and genuinely want to. The problem is that when you're supporting someone who is, for example, experiencing thoughts of suicide, or who has had past attempts, the crisis doesn't just last a few hours. It may be days, weeks, months, or even years, with small moments of respite along the way. So yes, you can go overtime for a client in crisis, take extra care checking in with them between sessions, or even walk with them to the hospital emergency room if needed. But at some point, and I hate to be so obvious, you're going to have to go to the bathroom. You're going to need to go get a glass of water. You're also eventually going to need to eat, and sleep, and shower, and potentially go to work or take care of your kids (if you have those things). At some point, you're going to need to leave the person alone. You simply cannot be there all the time.

Now, before you start thinking about how you're going to manage to take your client to the bathroom with you, remember that doing so is not just impractical; it is undesirable for both of you. No one likes to feel that they are being constantly monitored, that they can't be trusted, or that they're dependent on others. Treating people in these ways often leads them to resentment.

It goes the other way too. Most people I meet are pretty generous with their time, but when taking care of others starts to get in the way of their self-nurturance, it doesn't matter how much they believe it's the "right" thing to do: they get resentful. So yes, we might like to be there for someone one-hundred percent. We might even believe that's a great thing to do. But we also need to recognize that we aren't actually capable of doing it. Having limits is simply part of being alive, and respecting those limits is essential to traversing life on this planet, especially if we want that life to be a contented one.

The Boundaried Therapist is a contemporary, interactive guide for therapists about setting personal boundaries that will help them develop a practice and, importantly, a *life* that is sustainable, joyful, and energetic. I include in the term *therapist* professional space-holders of all kinds: psychologists, social workers, counsellors, coaches, psychotherapists, psychiatrists, and more. I draw on a range of works about boundaries, some that speak directly to the counselling profession, many that come out of other areas of thought and practice, and all of which share wisdom about boundaries that can support therapists in their practices. I encourage readers to take what I share as offerings rather than ultimate truth; I do not believe in a one-size-fits-all approach, and I do not find it helpful to offer prescriptions for other people's boundaries. I encourage self-reflection (a process that, alongside quality, process-oriented supervision, many psychologists report to be vital to their self-care[2]), and I am guided by an approach informed by feminist, somatic, and experiential practices. I have found that tuning into ourselves, our bodies, and our own nervous systems tends to open us to answers that others simply cannot provide us: answers to what we need and what we cannot abide as individuals.

It has been important to me to approach this book with the same collaborative, feminist worldview I take with my clients and supervisees. For me, this means underlining that I am not writing from a neutral or unbiased perspective. I endeavour to minimize my biases by including solid research and diverse voices, but I do come to this from a particular point of view and set of life experiences. I am a white Canadian settler woman and a millennial. Throughout my upbringing, I mostly learned how to be nice and work hard (but not how to rest, assert myself, or be satisfied with something that was "good enough"). I bring my identities as a feminist, mother, migraineur, psychologist, supervisor, and friend to both my clinical work and my writing. I have a background in crisis work, which pairs with my current experience in private practice. I have worked in group homes and shelters, on crisis lines, and at sexual assault centres. In my years of caring for others in a professional capacity, I've been able to enjoy deep, rich, loving experiences with many people who've been brave enough to share their lives with me. I wrote this book from a place of wanting to provide tools and reassurance for other therapists, both preservice and practising, which they can use to shed old, destructive messages that say "Everyone else before you," and to grab hold of the life they desire.

This book offers you space to slow down and attune to your boundaries, let go of guilt, and get clear on what you need to sustain you as a person first, then as a therapist. Part I looks at the concept of boundaries generally, and how it applies to therapists specifically. In the first chapter, I offer my own understanding of boundaries. I also guide you through exercises designed to help you release beliefs about boundaries that are no longer serving you and to adopt new ones. In chapter 2, I cover some occupational hazards of counselling professions—burnout, vicarious trauma, and resentment— and explore how boundaries can help avoid these life-altering and sometimes career-ending outcomes. Chapter 3 looks specifically at embodied decision-making: a somatic-experience-based practice aimed at learning to act in line with your needs and values. Then, in chapter 4, I do a deep dive into how guilt shows up for therapists, and how we can move through it.

The remaining chapters make up part II of the book. There, I explore boundary-setting for therapists in three general, work-related domains: emotions, time and attention, and workplace and finances. These chapters take a closer look at some of the day-to-day areas in which many therapists struggle to set boundaries, offering some practical ideas about where to begin.

On certain topics, I've invited colleagues to share their first-person perspectives about boundaries from their experiences in the profession. Throughout the book, you'll also find reflection questions that invite you to begin exploring, recognizing, and honouring your own perspective and your own needs.

My commitment in this book is to help you notice what your capacity is and to get clear on what nourishes you. Boundaries are about so much more than understanding and enforcing our nos. *They are also about making room for our yeses.* At its heart, that is what this book is really about: learning to say yes to what sustains you, what makes you feel alive, what aligns with your values, and what keeps you grounded. Finding and nurturing your yeses with boundaries that align with your needs and values as a human being will help you remain connected not only with your clients but with yourself. Both types of connection are key to sustaining a vibrant counselling practice for many years to come. My vision is that this book helps you position your work as a fulfilling and satisfying part of your life, but not as the whole thing. Remember: you are a human first, a therapist second.

PART I

Rethinking Boundaries

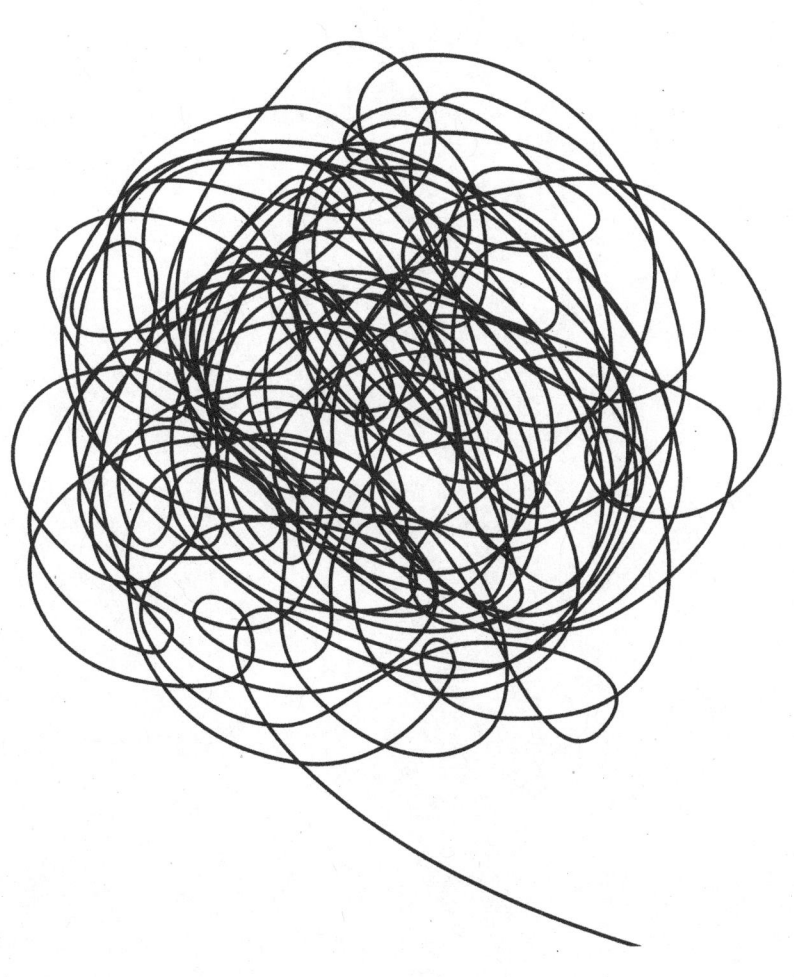

1

Boundaries Make Room for Yes

One of the lessons I have learned from living with pain is that time is not a guarantee. In my first year of dealing with migraines, I often only had a few hours each day to focus on something other than managing my pain. Those few hours became very precious. I wanted to make the most of the pain-free time I did have, and to engage in things that really brought me joy. I very quickly got clear on what was truly important to me and what was "extra." I also very quickly learned that, to show up for my family, friends, and clients, I also had to show up for myself. Setting clear boundaries became integral to giving myself the time I needed to nurture myself so I could nurture others.

In North America, we live in a society that deemphasizes the importance of and even discourages boundaries. (We'll touch on this again in chapter 4.) Most of us have been taught that turning toward ourselves is selfish because it takes away from the time and energy we give to other people. Directly and indirectly, we've been made to feel like the care we do give others isn't enough—like we can always turn further away from ourselves, and that this turning away will allow us to turn towards others even more. These messages are often amplified in counselling professions.

Many therapists have been led to believe that boundaries get in the way of them doing what they are trained to do: help others by connecting with them on a human level. Boundaries, it is thought, are about closing oneself off to others in order to focus on ourselves. They are rules we set up to protect ourselves from other people. This belief may be held alongside another: that the only way to connect with others is to open one's whole heart to them in an unbounded way, or to be available to help them in as many ways as possible. Can I take on another client in my already busy schedule? Yes. Can I field calls from struggling clients in my off-hours? Yes. Can I take an appointment during my lunch break because it's the only time my client can see me this week? Yes. This is what helping *means* to many therapists: saying yes to others and no to ourselves.

When we take these two beliefs together, it's easy to see why therapists struggle to set boundaries. If helping is about unlimited openness and connection to others, and boundaries are about cutting ourselves off from connection with others, then boundaries are antithetical to helping, and certainly to helping professions. I believe that these understandings of helping and boundaries, and how they relate to one another, cause us to lose sight of a key ingredient of human relations: that they are an (at least) two-way street.

When we understand boundaries as solid barriers that protect us from other people, we frame them in the negative. They are well-defined points, often right at if not slightly past our point of exhaustion, at which we say no to the requests of others. I prefer, instead, to frame boundaries in the positive: boundaries are about identifying our yeses as much as, if not more than, our nos. Instead of being rigid rules that state what I am not willing to do for others, boundaries help me connect with what I *am* willing to do, today, or for this person, or in this particular situation. "Yes" boundaries help me make true connections with others by helping me connect with myself. When I talk about boundaries in this book, I talk about them primarily in terms of this second meaning.

Boundaries Are Reflections of Our Needs

The boundaries we set reflect the needs that we have. As I often say, our boundaries are the external expression of our internal limits. I created this definition a number of years ago and continue to use it in my work every day. If, for example, you are feeling emotionally tired, you may have come up against a limit in your emotional capacity. You might respond by doing something rejuvenating: seeing a good friend, going on a long hike, taking a nap, or whatever it is that fills your cup. This act is an expression of your internal limit. It says, "I'm out of batteries for emotional work today. I need to stop doing that work and instead do something to charge my batteries again." Take another example: You feel anxious about leading a meeting for the first time. You might express that limit as a boundary by asking for emotional support or advice from a colleague. Or again, perhaps you're feeling overwhelmed because your workload is too heavy. You might express that limit as a boundary by having a conversation with your supervisor about expectations and priorities. Notice that in each example, the boundary is not a rule to follow—"I can't do anything that makes me too emotionally exhausted, too nervous, too overwhelmed"—but an action to take that will support your well-being and help you do the things you want or need to do: refreshing your emotional energy with an activity you love so you can use that energy in your work and life, seeking emotional support so you can feel more confident doing something you're nervous about, communicating your needs with others to find a way to work more sustainably, or choosing to take some things off your plate so you can focus on your priorities. Boundaries are expressions of our internal limits because they are the actions we do for ourselves to meet our own needs.

> ## Reflect and Journal
> - Think of a time you felt a limit or identified a need for yourself. How did you respond? How did this response line up with the limit you felt or the need you identified?
> - Imagine you look at your calendar for the coming week and notice that you've been booked in with clients over your lunch hours, overstepping your need to have a break and eat. How might you express your limit?

Many counselling professionals report that they want to be able to keep doing their work but are so overwhelmed and consumed by it that their energy is deteriorating. Feelings of resentment, overwhelm, and burnout are usually signs that our limits have been crossed and it's time to set a boundary (more on this in chapter 2). For therapists working under the understanding that helping others requires unbounded openness, coming up against their personal limits can feel devastating. Feeling overwhelmed may seem like a sign that they aren't good enough helpers; being burnt out might make them feel they don't have what it takes. I don't believe this. Having boundaries around your work is not a reflection of you as a person, nor of your dedication to or skill at the work. It is instead a reflection of your needs as a human being.

Tricia Hersey, author of *Rest is Resistance* and founder of The Nap Ministry, encourages us to embrace rest as a form of liberation. In one post, she reminds us that the need for rest touches everyone, even those of us who love our work: "You can really, really love the work you do, see it as a calling, be super grateful for all the opportunities coming your way, AND still need a break and be exhausted from it."[1]

I think we all need a break from the work of helping others every now and again. This doesn't mean this work is not for us or that someone else would be better suited to it. It just means that we are human. We have boundaries because we have limits and needs, and we have limits and needs because we are human.

In my practice, I often talk about needs. Yet it's not just needs but wants that are human, and wants deserve space, too.[2] For example, I may not *need* a workplace that's within biking distance, but I sure do want that! It can be so affirming to get in touch with our wants and desires, and to begin to imagine how good this work could be. Boundaries can help with this, too. Practising boundaries helps us say yes to what brings us life, to what we care about, and to what matters to us.

Just how do we get in touch with our wants and needs? If you've grown up in a predominantly Western culture, you may be used to *thinking* about a question like this and reasoning your way to an answer. When it comes to knowing what we want or need in a particular situation, however, this can produce somewhat limited results: It's possible to effectively argue two opposing positions and to feel intellectually convinced by both of them. But what happens when we turn toward how our bodies *feel* about those same two positions? You may have heard the saying "The body doesn't lie." I find a lot of truth in this. In my work as a somatic therapist, I often encourage clients to understand their needs by consciously tuning into the signals from their heads, hearts, and bodies—their intellectual, emotional, and physical wisdom—and striving to honour all of that wisdom together. I call this *embodied decision-making*, and we'll explore it further in chapter 3.

Know that it's normal to be unsure of exactly what your wants and needs are. Beginning to sort this out is one of the things we'll focus on in this book. As an opening exercise, consider trying what Ariel Gore suggests: Give yourself one uninterrupted day to explore your needs and wants without judgment:

> Allow yourself to follow the day wherever it takes you. Allow yourself to become mesmerized by the flow of events, by the uninterruptedness of it all.
>
> …If you meant to spend your day climbing a mountain and instead found yourself reading a thick novel at the funky café with the elk head mounted on the wall, do not decide, on your way home, that you have been lazy. It doesn't matter. You can climb the mountain next time. Or not.[3]

The flexibility of Gore's approach in this exercise teaches two important facts about our wants and needs: They can change moment to moment, and we are allowed to shift our decisions and the ways we move through life along with them. Yet it's normal, too, to not know how to give yourself permission to listen for and fulfil your wants and needs. In their book *Journal of Radical Permission*, activists adrienne maree brown and Sonya Renee Taylor describe this type of permission-giving as a radical act—something that goes against the grain.[4] It can feel scary to give ourselves permissions that we've never given before, and that we've never known we *could* give. As brown envisions for us, however, when you give yourself permission to pursue your wants and needs, "you feel free from within, you embody freedom for and with others, and you raise the bar of connection in your life to that of liberatory relationships."[5] Boundaries, at their core, are this kind of radical permission.

Reflect and Journal

- When it comes to how work fits into your life, what do you most want? What do you need?
- What does it feel like to honour your wants and needs as valid, even if you don't yet know how to meet them?

Questions inspired by Lisa Olivera, "July Journaling Guide," *Human Stuff*, July 3, 2022, https://lisaolivera.substack.com/p/july-journaling-guide.

Boundaries Are Not Rules

In *More Than Two*, Franklin Veaux and Eve Rickert differentiate between boundaries and rules. Rules, they note, are other-focused. They are about trying to exert control over someone else's choices or behaviours. By contrast, boundaries are self-focused. They are about the things I can control in myself: my choices and my behaviours. Sometimes the two can be hard to distinguish, especially because it isn't so hard to state them both in "I" language, but it's not just about language here. As Rickert and Veaux explain, the way to distinguish a boundary from a rule is to pay attention to the way you feel when another person does not behave in a way that is conducive to that boundary or rule.

Let's say you've made it clear in your consent forms that you are not able to provide therapy outside of clients' scheduled sessions, including by telephone or over email. You have a client who repeatedly emails you outside of their session time with detailed information and questions, and clearly expects you to respond. How do you respond to this? If the situation leads you to focus on how to make your client stop emailing you, your response will likely be a rule more than it is a boundary. Rules can be challenging to navigate in a therapeutic relationship. In worst-case scenarios, when a client breaks a rule we have set, it can lead us to view their behaviour as disrespectful and cause us to have a harder time extending empathy. These issues may ultimately spell the end of the therapeutic relationship.

If, however, the statement in your consent form is truly a boundary, you'll notice that your focus is not on how wrong the client was to behave as they did but on your own feelings and the next steps you need to take. You might notice your own disappointment and then focus on what you need to do next. Next steps may involve resisting the urge to reply by email, gently reaffirming your boundaries to the client when you see them in person, and redirecting them to alternative crisis resources. If the client continues to be unable to respect your boundaries, you'll continue asking yourself what you need to do to help *yourself* navigate the situation. Depending on the situation, you may eventually need to terminate the therapeutic relationship.

Notice how the rule-oriented example and the boundary-oriented example both have the potential to lead to the same result: terminating the relationship. Consider, though, that when you are truly prioritizing a boundary, this type of decision is not about punishing the other person or hoping that that they'll change their behaviour. Instead, prioritizing a boundary is about getting clear on your own expectations and needs in the job of serving others. It's about mustering the courage to acknowledge when a situation is not a good fit. I love how clearly Rickert and Veaux make this point: "The key with boundaries is that you always set them around those things that are *yours*: your body, your mind, your emotions, your time, intimacy with you. You *always* have a right to regulate access to what is yours."[6]

Harriet Lerner, in her book *The Dance of Anger*, likewise reminds us that boundaries are not about changing someone else's behaviour: "We cannot make another person change his or her steps to an old dance, but if we change our own steps, the dance no longer can continue in the same predictable pattern."[7] If you've been trying to set boundaries and are feeling frustrated with the result, consider checking in with yourself about whether you're in fact trying to change someone else (but please, be compassionate with yourself as you reflect—many of us can inadvertently get caught up in these kinds of patterns). If you find the answer is yes, then ask yourself, as Lerner puts it, how to begin changing "your own steps."

How *does* one learn to set boundaries instead of rules? The short answer is "It takes practice." We need to practice identifying, listening to, and honouring our own needs. You may find as you work on boundaries that you've been acting out of sync with your internal sense of what's best for you, and of what you need. This is not surprising. Many of us have been taught in so many ways and for so long to ignore our needs; in this, we are well practiced. Over time, the practice of ignoring our needs teaches us to tune out the emotional and somatic messages we send ourselves about those needs, but that doesn't mean we're tuning everything out. It's important to recognize that when we're not listening to ourselves about our needs, we may well be listening to someone else: We may be basing our decisions about and assessments of our own needs and limits on what other people value or believe, and this doesn't tend to work out very well. Doing something incongruous with our values solely to please another person is dissatisfying at best. Over time, it can also leave us feeling trapped, powerless, and unable to make choices aligned with joy or our own life purpose. Fortunately, it is never too late to practice listening to ourselves again, or listening better, despite all the practice we've had doing otherwise.

> ## Reflect and Journal
> Think of a time you've set a rule instead of a boundary. Acknowledge the protective parts of you that were trying to keep you safe. Now ask yourself: How could you change this rule into a boundary?

Boundaries Are a Practice

When I say that boundaries are a practice, I mean that there is no failsafe script that every person can use in every situation to set a boundary. Boundaries are unique to each of us, and they are not static: they will change as we change over the course of our lives. Although it can be difficult to feel like there's no one "right way" to set and practice boundaries, most of the clients and supervisees I work with find that a more personal, individualized practice is ultimately more freeing.

The boundaries we each set for ourselves are informed by our upbringings, our cultures, our identities, our experiences, our present situations, and our goals. Our limits and needs are unique to us because we each have our own unique story. For these reasons, the boundaries we set and how we practice them really will look different for each of us.

Imagine, for example, a situation that has come up more than once in my conversations with other therapists: a white therapist working with a BIPOC client who is experiencing challenges in their romantic and family life. The therapist talks to the client about relationship codependency and about how they may care too much about what their family thinks of their actions. In this situation, the therapist may frame conversations about boundaries around values from their own culture: that relationships shouldn't be codependent, and people shouldn't care too much about what their family thinks. The therapist assumes that these firm boundaries are the equivalent of "healthy" boundaries for everyone. The client, coming from a collectivist cultural perspective, may not feel that such firm boundaries around family and relationships fit their needs or desires, and may feel judged, pressured, or pathologized by the therapist's narrow view of boundary-setting according to individualist culture expectations.[8]

This example takes an intercultural perspective, and offers an important reminder: While connection is essential to all of us for survival, it will be prioritized even more in cultures whose very identities have been threatened. The example also illustrates a fundamental truth about boundaries that applies to everyone: You can't set them for other people based on those you have for yourself because you are not in a position to know what will truly respond to the limits and needs of others. Conversely, only you can identify which boundaries work for you, because only you can feel when you need to say no and when your whole self says yes.

When it comes to setting boundaries, my colleague Sholly Scarlett suggests asking some questions: Why am I following this? Who put this in place? and especially, Does this align with who I am? For this last question, Sholly finds that if she is following a boundary from the dominant culture, often it doesn't. She explains that, for example, while avoiding dual relationships (any situations where dual roles exist between a therapist and a client) is an accepted dominant approach in therapy, this is not as realistic in the Black community. Black therapists are likely to see their clients outside the therapy room, whether at church, community events, or elsewhere. While this may have its challenges, it can also build trust. Black clients may be more likely to reach out for support if it's with someone they've seen before and can identify as part of the community. Sholly notes that when she softened her boundaries in ways that were more culturally aligned, the relationship became more therapeutic. To help ensure she's still abiding by ethical guidelines, she constantly checks in with her colleagues about her approach. Striking this balance, Sholly says, has allowed her to feel more abundant in her practice: "I find I'm not as black and white anymore. I'm colourful."

First-Person Perspectives

We should always ask ourselves who is defining what an acceptable boundary is in a work context, and understand that power, privilege, and cultural roles are also at play in boundary-setting. Imagine a Black psychologist who has come to Canada as an immigrant and had to re-take their graduate education because their masters or doctoral degree was not accepted by the College of Psychologists of their province. Once they are working as a psychologist again, they work late or take work home to complete.

> From the outside, through a white, individualistic, North American lens, a colleague may see this Black psychologist as having "poor boundaries." The Black psychologist, however, may see the "extra" that they do for their job as "what they need to do to survive," based on their past and ongoing struggle to have to prove themselves in a white-dominant culture, including getting back the career that they had already worked for. Always consider by whose standards boundaries are defined.
> —*Sophia C. Parks, Registered Psychologist*

Boundaries change from situation to situation and over the course of our lives. As we go through life changes, we may desire a change in role or work environment. Becoming a parent, for example, can change our needs, and therefore our boundaries, at work. In one study on Canadian psychologist mothers, some participants shared that they felt they needed greater flexibility in their work schedule after becoming a parent. For some mothers working for an employer, this need motivated them to move to private practice where they could better control their work hours. Participants who became parents while already in private practice also noticed changes in their needs, and some noted the downsides of private practice when it came to responding to those needs—for instance, that they didn't have access to health benefits or parental leave.[9] What worked for these psychologists prior to parenthood didn't always work as well afterwards.

Boundaries can even change over the course of the week as we cope with the ups and downs of daily life and the circumstances in which we experience those ups and downs. If you have a supportive colleague at work, for instance, it might feel easier to set limits at work; when that person is on holiday, you might find that it becomes more difficult. What we can offer and where our limits are also vary according to our emotional and physical state at any particular moment. For example, your ability to be present and attuned with clients may depend on how recently you've eaten. Personally, my ability to take on an extra hour of work depends on whether I'm experiencing pain that day.

Some therapists may also notice at some point that work that was once fulfilling is no longer a good fit. Sometimes this realization may motivate a change of workplace or the type of services a person offers. Other times, it may motivate someone to not to be a therapist anymore. Our deepest needs and wants can change even when we aren't expecting them to, and that's okay. Many of us imagine our future in a particular way and then have it unfold quite differently. When this happens, it doesn't mean we've failed or done something wrong. Responding to our new needs doesn't mean "quitting" or "giving up." I like to think of it, instead, as changing course.

Just as having needs is a human reality, so is the fact that those needs will change, and as we change and grow, so do our boundaries.

Boundaries are a practice because we never learn, once and for all, how to "do" them. Practising boundaries is not a journey of perfection or avoiding pain, and it will regularly involve making mistakes, re-evaluating, and trying again. It also involves communicating with others who have their own histories, needs, and boundaries. Even when we're doing right by ourselves, it doesn't mean we can escape the realities of being a human in relationship with other humans: When we practice boundaries, we will disappoint others, despite our best efforts not to. This practice therefore requires self-compassion. As counselling professionals, we need to be kind to ourselves and tend to our own needs like we tend to the needs of others.

First-Person Perspectives

Former therapist Lisa Olivera shares her experience of coming up against a boundary in her own career path after becoming a parent, and ultimately deciding to step away from therapy.

It was a decision I didn't anticipate when returning from maternity leave four months ago; I imagined myself itching with eagerness to be doing something other than mothering again, to be in conversation with other adults, to be holding space for something other than the entirely unpredictable feelings of a new baby. And to be honest, I thought I had to—I didn't feel there was an option to choose to stop. No longer working as a therapist seemed like it was out of the question.

I soon realized (my body told me before my brain did): holding space for others in that specific way just wasn't going to work for me in this season of life, for so many reasons. I wanted it to work. I wanted to be able to — the thought of such a big transition, of no longer holding the title so many people see me as, of ending with many clients I had for years, of not having a back-up plan, was terrifying to me.

And, along with that want, there was the *reality*. I have been woven up in depression that postpartum didn't make easier. I have been so, so tired. I have been unable to keep in touch with friends and family. I have been figuring out how to be a mom, how to adjust to a completely life-altering transition, how to find myself after losing the version that existed before. And within all of this, I simply had nothing left. I had no more space to hold. I had no more energy to spare. And the work of therapy requires more of me than I have to give in this season. Beyond all that, I no longer had the desire to do 1:1 therapy work. And letting that be okay has been one of the biggest permission slips I've ever given myself.[10]

Boundaries Are Self-Care

Insofar as boundaries are about identifying and responding to our own needs and offering compassion to ourselves, they are a form of self-care.

I often hear people say, "I don't have enough time/energy/money to take care of myself." It's necessary to acknowledge that there are absolutely real barriers to contend with when it comes to self-care: Not everyone is in a position to sign up for a gym membership, buy organic food, go on vacation, or participate in many of the other typically cited self-care strategies. I know plenty of young parents who are short on time and plenty of single-income contract workers who are short on cash. We'll talk about this more in chapter 4. But many of us are also working within a narrative that we are not allowed to retreat and restore, or that we are not allowed to care for ourselves or be cared for. We may have a sense that other people have it worse than we do, and we therefore shouldn't prioritize ourselves. Just as we're rethinking boundaries, we also need to rethink self-care.

When I talk about self-care, I'm talking about any practice that nourishes you—that connects you to life and joy. Nourishing practices go hand in hand with boundaries because boundaries involve making more space for the things we want out of life. In the context of our work as therapists, if we want to bring our aliveness to a session or meeting with someone we're helping, we need to be connecting to our aliveness outside the session. Self-care may also be thought of as any strategy that helps us return to or expand our window of tolerance (figure 1.1). Coined by psychologist Dan Siegel, the *window of tolerance* is the range of emotional intensity or arousal in which a person can best function in their lives.[11] Stress can shrink our window or cause us to operate outside it, leading to experiences of dysregulation on two extremes: hyperarousal (which might look like anxiety, overwhelm, or agitation) and hypoarousal (which might look like spaciness, numbness, or emotional shutdown). Self-care activities can help us slow down and expand our window of tolerance or return us to its safe boundaries. Self-care can therefore include taking the space and time, when you are stressed, to reconnect with yourself and your body, and to ground yourself in your surroundings and the present moment.[12]

Many therapists have advocated that we view self-care as an ethical imperative, rather than an optional addition, to our work. This position is

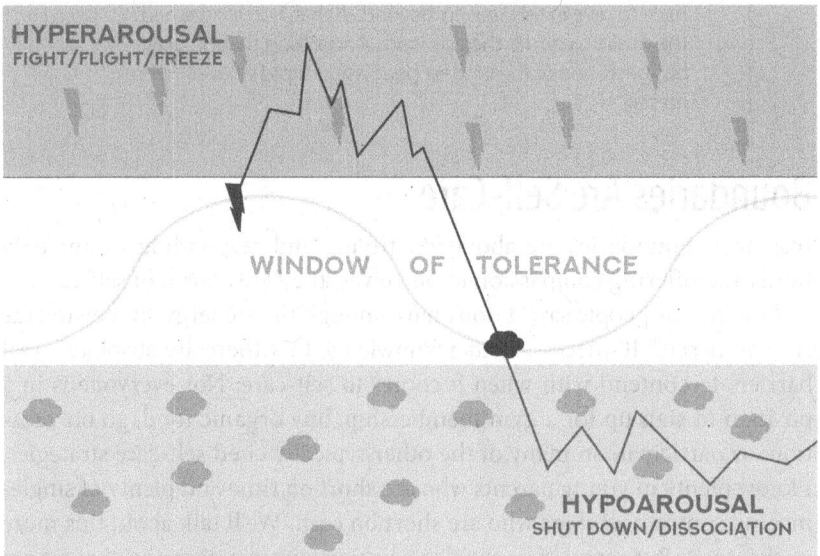

Figure 1.1 *The window of tolerance*

supported by the Canadian Code of Ethics for Psychologists, which states that psychologists must "engage in self-care activities that help to avoid conditions (e.g., burnout, addictions) that could result in impaired judgment and interfere with their ability to benefit and not harm others."[13] In other words, taking care of ourselves is one of our professional responsibilities.

One 2016 meta-analysis on graduate students showed that purposeful effort toward maintaining well-being (e.g., sleep, mindfulness, engaging in hobbies) increased self-compassion and life satisfaction and reduced stress and psychological distress. One interesting finding of this study was that "although self-care may alleviate…stress to some degree, it may do a better job at providing students with the tools to adaptively handle the stress."[14] That is, self-care may be less about ridding oneself of stress and more about having the tools to handle it when it arises. This is an important recognition because a certain level of stress in graduate school (and indeed, throughout one's career and life) will be unavoidable.

The results from the 2016 meta-analysis also indicated that the benefits of self-care were similar regardless of the type of self-care activity the students engaged in. This fits in with what we've already discussed: our needs and wants will be different from our neighbours, and we must check in with ourselves to notice and act on what nourishes us most. One person might benefit most from engaging in mindfulness while another will get the most out of consistent movement. When it comes to self-care, work on iden-tifying the activities that work best for you, regularly participate in those activities, and know that what works best now will likely change through the seasons of the year and the seasons of your life.

Boundaries Require Support

Turning inward to discover our needs also tends to reveal what outside sup-port we require. The term *self-care* emphasizes an individualistic idea of care, but most of us are not actually built to do this care alone: It takes time, money, and energy that are sometimes in short supply. Setting boundaries, in particular, involves confronting old beliefs, experiences of guilt, and the possibility of disappointing others and making mistakes—experiences that can be scary, taxing, and difficult to lean into alone, especially if they are new to us. Sustainably setting boundaries requires that we go beyond indi-vidualistic notions of self-care and recognizing that we all require networks of support, and we all rely on each other.

This is the idea behind community care, which community organizer Nakita Valerio defines as "people committed to leveraging their privilege to be there for one another in various ways."[15] Ultimately, community care means being part of a compassionate group of individuals who are commit-ted to supporting one another's needs to the best of their ability. We cannot, however, control what others are or are not willing and able to give us in terms of support. What we can do is ask our communities for what we need and know what compromises we're willing to make when our ideal support is not available. In the workplace, if help is not available within the limits of your compromises, it may be time to look for new support networks or to move on to a different position or workplace.

Community care within a workplace may look like access to supportive peers or to an on-site supervisor who can help you work through diffi-cult emotions and parse challenging situations, or it might mean working within a multidisciplinary team that understands and supports one other. It might involve having optional monthly lunches or a walking group to make time for connection. A workplace community might commit to having a scent-free facility because it's helpful to even one member, or it might look at bringing in outside training to support ongoing learning.

Community and peer support help people maintain boundaries, espe-cially in the context of avoiding burnout. Research has shown that hav-ing supportive supervisors and a compassionate peer group who can offer immediate support following a difficult session benefits therapists' well-being.[16] In one study on burnout and growth among Australian psychologists, all participants emphasized the importance of quality supervision that was self-reflective, process-oriented, and interpersonal.[17]

Preparing to Set New Boundaries

It's one thing to feel you need a boundary and another to know exactly what that boundary will be—what, exactly, you need or want to change, or what you're okay with changing. You may even feel unsure that you're allowed to set a boundary or make a change. These feelings can be difficult to manage and sorting them out will take time. For starters, remember that you *are* allowed to move on from situations that aren't working for you, and you *are* allowed to make changes in your current situation that serve you better. You are allowed to work toward respecting your limits while remaining in connection with others. To protect ourselves, our relationships, and our work, we need to. When you feel ready to start exploring new boundaries at work or in other parts of your life, a first step is to get clear on where you're starting from. Check in with yourself about your current boundaries and what is motivating you right now to do this work around boundary-setting.

Exercise: Mindfulness for Making Changes

The work of making changes can seem daunting and difficult to begin, even when a part of us wants to jump in. I encourage you to do what you need to bring the possibility of change within your reach. Start by getting clear on why you're doing it—not why other people think you should make a change, but what really drives you to do the difficult work of change. The following exercise is meant to help you begin to explore your why. You can do this exercise alone or with a partner, with your eyes open or closed—whatever's most comfortable for you.

I invite you to take a moment to get comfortable in your seat and turn your attention inward. I'd like you to connect with the part of you, deep inside, that wants to do this work on boundaries now. The part of you that knows the time is right, that knows this path is the one for you. It may be the part of you that's sick, and tired, and has to put your health as a priority. It may be the part of you that wants to keep giving to the people you love or work with and doesn't want to risk losing that. It may be the part of you that desires more energy, enthusiasm, and hope. Connect with that part of yourself now. Notice what happens in your body as you connect with that part of yourself. Notice how you hold this truth.

What is the emotion that tells you, "This is right"? What are the sensations associated with that emotion? Perhaps there's a feeling of being settled, relaxed, or at ease. Perhaps there's a warmth, lightness, or solid feeling. Perhaps there's something entirely different. Take the time to simply feel into this part of yourself and its wisdom.

A second step is to interrogate the patterned ways with which we've already been approaching boundaries, and then ask ourselves whether that approach really fits with our needs and personal limits. This means turning inward and understanding where your strengths around boundaries are, and where you struggle. Think of your boundaries as existing on a continuum, with one side representing the parts of yourself that are good at being firm, and the other side containing the parts that are good at being flexible. This strengths-based, non-pathologizing view of boundaries allows us to view all our patterned behaviours as adaptations to life's challenges. The key is noticing where your answers show up on the boundaries continuum, and if there's room for new behaviours to arise.

Reflect and Journal

- What motivates you to work on boundaries, even when it's hard?
- What is the smallest piece of evidence that would help you feel that the work you're doing around boundaries is meaningful, even when it's hard?

Exercise: Boundary Continuums

For the purpose of this exercise, we're going to focus on work-related boundaries, though if you choose, you could repeat the exercise in other areas of your life.

In your journal, draw a horizontal line from one side of the page to the other. On one end of the line, write "good at being firm"; on the other end, write "good at being flexible." Next, mark out where you land on the continuum between firm to flexible in the following boundary categories: emotional (you can mark both what you take on *and* what you take in), time, and financial.

Once you've marked out how firm or flexible your boundaries are in each category, take time to reflect. First, simply see what you notice. Is there a pattern to your continuum? Then, ask yourself if there's anything you'd like to change. You may want to invite more openness in certain situations, and you may want more of a protective barrier in others. It's up to you to choose what's best for

you. There's no need to actually change anything just yet—simply
notice where you might want to see change.

I strongly encourage people to actually mark their behaviours and adaptations down on a visual continuum like in the exercise above. In addition to understanding where you tend to land on the continuum (and how
where you tend to land might change depending on what kind of boundary
you're tracking), you also want to be able to look at the whole picture. Most
people who struggle with boundaries around work (and boundaries in general) find that their boundaries tend to cluster at one end of the continuum
or the other, or at extreme ends with nothing in the middle. Getting a sense
of what your continuum looks like can tell an important story.

And of course, it's important to remember that your boundaries are not
written in stone. Just because you marked a boundary on your continuum
as "flexible" doesn't mean that it will be perfectly flexible in every situation.
There is no one right boundary for everybody in every situation, even if it's
a boundary we've set for ourselves. As we've discussed, boundary practice
begins not by setting ourselves rules to follow but by asking ourselves some
important questions:

- What am I willing and able to give?
- What do I need?
- What supports and nourishes me?

Regularly asking ourselves these
questions, even if we aren't yet sure
how to go about answering them,
will help us begin to create respon-
sive and adaptive boundaries for
ourselves.

Some nervousness or discomfort
when setting boundaries is normal,
but your discomfort should not be
so overwhelming that it's out of your
window of tolerance. Let yourself get to a point where, even if you're not
perfectly relaxed, calm, and cool about the whole process, you're still ready
enough to handle the potential push-back that may come from others, and
even from within yourself. This might mean gathering your strength first,
or working with a therapist of your own so you feel more resourced to handle what happens in the aftermath.

When you do feel ready to set a new boundary, start small. Making huge
changes all at once can be overwhelming for our nervous systems. It's easy

Reflect and Journal

Write about a time where one of
your work-related boundaries felt
too flexible or too firm for you. How
do you know within yourself that
the boundary you put in place in
that situation was not quite right
for you at the time?

to get so excited about the prospect of setting boundaries that you swing from one end of the continuum to the other; it doesn't take much push-back to swing back to the other side again. So start small, and then prac-tise, practise, practise. I hear again and again from those I work with that boundaries get easier with time. Consider practising your new boundary in a situation that feels safe to you first, perhaps with a therapist or a really supportive friend or colleague who will be more than accepting of a no from you—someone who will help you understand that it's okay to say no, and that no doesn't automatically lead to disconnection. Having this kind of support can help boost our confidence and let us see that there are people in our lives who want to be around us regardless of what we do or don't do for them. As we practice more, any guilt around having boundaries tends to dissipate, and we can even feel proud of ourselves for meeting our own needs. We grow more confident in our own abilities, and we start to discern the aspects of our lives that are working for us (those that help us abide by our boundaries) and those that might not be a good fit anymore.

There's no one perfect way to set boundaries—just the way that works best for you. Whatever that is, you figure it out with time and practice.

Boundary Practice

Assemble a support network for yourself—a team of people you can trust. This may include several people who can support you personally, such as a good friend, partner, or therapist. It should also include people who can support you professionally, such as a co-worker or supervisor who shares your values.

2

Boundaries Sustain Us

Avoiding Burnout, Vicarious Trauma, and Resentment as a Therapist

I want all of us, as therapists, to be able to name what our comfort levels are. I want us to feel like it's okay to have needs and to put them on the table. Most of all, I want us to know that we're not being a problem by doing so. We can accomplish these things by setting boundaries.

A lot of what I share about boundaries can be helpful for anyone, therapist or not, but therapists in particular need to think about boundaries because of the emotionally demanding work we do. We are at special risk for burnout and vicarious trauma, and pushing ourselves past our limits can lead to resentment that interferes with our willingness and ability to keep doing our work.

In my practice as a therapist, boundaries continually come up as a protective and sustaining factor. For this reason, we should think about the work of understanding our needs and setting boundaries not as extra, but as an essential part of our work. Boundaries help us cope with the impacts of repeated occupational exposure to trauma and suffering and allow us to safely and ethically continue our work as therapists. Boundaries can help us heal from harm that we are already experiencing, but they are, importantly, also a form of *proactive* self-care. They can help us avoid many of the possible negative outcomes of our work in the first place.

Unfortunately, despite our professional responsibilities, personal boundaries are rarely a topic of serious and substantial discussion in therapist training.[1] So let's start that discussion.

Boundaries Protect Us

Boundaries sustain us by protecting us from the occupational hazards of our work. Three of the most common hazards for therapists are burnout, vicarious trauma, and resentment.

Burnout

Many psychologists will be familiar with burnout as a serious psychological health issue. In 2019, the World Health Organization officially recognized burnout as an occupational phenomenon, and the International Classification of Diseases included it in its eleventh edition. Since then, workers in many industries, including therapists, have come to understand the signs of burnout and the importance of attending to them.

We can think of burnout as "exhaustion-plus." As Anne Helen Petersen, author of *Can't Even: How Millennials Became the Burnout Generation*, puts it, "Exhaustion means going to the point where you can't go any further; burnout means reaching that point and pushing yourself to keep going, whether for days or weeks or years."[2] In the counselling profession, burnout is neither rare nor easy to recover from. A 2018 study on Canadian psychotherapists found that 20 percent of psychotherapists were emotionally exhausted and 10 percent were in a state of significant psychological distress.[3] Despite the high rates of burnout in our profession, relatively little research has explored the lived experience of burnout in psychologists,[4] and many psychologists I've surveyed have felt that they do not have sufficient training to recognize burnout in themselves or to implement strategies to protect themselves from it.

Social psychologist Christina Maslach and her collaborators define burnout as a mental, emotional, and physical condition with three central characteristics:
1. Emotional exhaustion (the individual stress response)
2. Cynicism (the negative reaction to others and the job)
3. A sense of inefficacy (the negative evaluation of one's own effectiveness)[5]

The condition stems from chronically high stress levels that wear on us over months, sometimes years. When our bodies perceive a stressor or threat, they protect us by releasing the stress hormone cortisol, which increases blood sugar and slows down nonessential functions (including our diges-tive and reproductive systems).[6] Our protective responses are activated, pri-oritizing survival over "rest and digest" functions of the parasympathetic nervous system. This response is incredibly helpful to get us through short-lived high-stress or crisis situations. Problems arise, however, when that high-stress or crisis state continues for longer periods of time. Our rest and digest functions aren't able to work as optimally as they should, which can lead to increased depression and anxiety, insomnia, digestive issues, and compromised immunity.[7] Elevated cortisol also leads to increased blood pressure, which raises the risk of heart attack and stroke over the long term.[8]

Writer Tiana Clark reminds us that burnout is nothing new. Black peo-ple and other marginalized groups have been tired for generations. But for Clark, the exhaustion she faces as a racialized woman is rooted in constant fear of financial and physical harm: worry that setting boundaries may cost her her livelihood or her life. She concludes that burnout for white, upper-middle-class workers is taxing mentally, but it's doubly so for marginalized folks who have to constantly prove their identity inside and outside the workplace.[9]

We should also consider that many folks with disabilities experience higher risk of burnout from constant effort to fit into an ableist, neurotypi-cal world.[10] Neurodivergent therapists have brought to light the exhaustion involved in constantly masking (attempting to blend in or hide the struggles they have, which often requires immense effort to suppress self-regulatory behaviors). One colleague of mine, Hannah, described struggling with time-blindness, constant fatigue, and insecurity about her neurodivergence that often led her to taking on more projects than she had capacity. All of this together left her constantly feeling on the edge of burnout: "These everyday struggles have cascading effects of lost productivity, procras-tination because doing anything feels very daunting, difficulty with self-motivation, and inner shame that as a therapist, I haven't 'figured it out' yet."

It's essential to take an intersectional lens whenever we talk about the barriers to setting boundaries—I'll delve into this more in chapter 4—but I hope it's also clear that the intricacies of combatting burnout apply uni-versally. For one, burnout can be difficult to anticipate in ourselves; its development is gradual, and thus hard to detect. As mental health writer Jill Dahl puts it in her article "Warning: 'Hanging in There' Is Destroying Your Health," "We get tricked into thinking that our lifestyle isn't catching up with us."[11] It isn't uncommon to miss symptoms of burnout in yourself until they have already triggered disease, so learning about and watching for the early signs is especially important. While everyone's signs will be different, common clues that you're getting burnt out include sleeplessness, irritability, lack of motivation, frequent illness, forgetfulness, and low energy.[12] Remember that burnout can affect different aspects of your life and can manifest physically (e.g., headaches, tension in shoulders, jaw, or stomach), behaviourally (e.g., numbing behaviours like drinking alcohol, scrolling through social media, or watching TV more than usual), mentally (e.g., spiraling thoughts, wondering what the point is, asking yourself if the work you do matters), and emotionally (e.g., feeling irritable, sad, or hopeless). When checking in on yourself, make sure you spend some time attending to all four areas.

Identifying Burnout

Consider using a standardized measure of burnout to help you identify burnout in yourself.

Available for a fee
- **Maslach Burnout Inventory (MBI).** Developed by Christina Maslach and Susan E. Jackson, this is the first scientifically developed measure of burnout, widely used in research, and aligns with the definition of burnout outlined earlier.

Available for free
- **Professional Quality of Life Scale (ProQol).** This measure was designed for helping professions to be able to assess three areas: compassion satisfaction, secondary traumatic stress, and burnout.

Certain personal factors, including high internal expectations and difficulty maintaining boundaries, make some people more susceptible to burnout that others; we'll talk more about these in other chapters. But burnout doesn't result from personal factors alone: it comes from the interaction of personal factors

Reflect and Journal

Take some time to reflect on what tends to burn you out most in your work as therapist. What's adding most to your burden right now? What is one thing that you can do this way to alleviate it?

with world factors, work factors, and the culture of psychology and the counselling profession more broadly. Numerous studies have shown that the work environment is a prominent factor in assessing risk for burnout,[13] and job demands such as hours worked, time spent in administrative paperwork, and negative client behaviours correlate to higher levels of burnout.[14] Maslach highlights six major work-related causes of burnout: work overload, lack of control, insufficient rewards, breakdown of workplace community, absence of fairness, and value conflict.[15] Work overload, in particular, continues to emerge as a strong predictor of burnout; this happens when a person's workload exceeds the time, energy, or resources they have available. Note that these factors can be present in any job, whether you love it or not; counter to the adage "If you love your job, you'll never work a day in your life," landing your dream job or doing work that you're passionate about will not suddenly make you immune to experiences of burnout. To avoid burnout, you need to find a work environment in which you are able to perform within your limits.

For many of the counsellors I work with, the experience of burnout leaves them so depleted that it affects their well-being even after they make a change or exit the situation that's burning them out. This is important to acknowledge because it's easy to get caught in thinking that it's okay to keep pushing past our limits, and that once we get out of a difficult situation, everything will be back to normal. We can't heal or avoid burnout simply by tacking on a fun activity at the end of our week. We need to set boundaries around how much of ourselves we are truly willing and able to give in the first place. Take a moment to think about what, exactly, most depletes you at work. For some, it's not one particular task, but the workload itself that makes the biggest difference. For others, certain administrative tasks, presenting issues, or client presentations may burn you out more than others. Once you know where the problem is, you can start to take steps to set boundaries. Those boundaries might look like reducing client load, delegating administrative tasks, referring certain issues out—whatever will start to give you more space and flexibility in the area that is causing you undue stress.

Because burnout can be so closely tied to workplace factors, and because many of these factors are outside of our immediate control (more on this in chapter 4), avoiding workplace burnout can be particularly challenging. This is where boundaries play an essential role. Boundaries can help us to get clear about what we are and are not able to abide at our jobs, and to make work-related decisions that start from that clarity. We'll talk more about workplace boundaries in chapter 8.

Reflect and Journal

- Have you experienced burnout before? What did the experience teach you about your own limits?
- Are you burnt out now? Do you recognize any of Maslach's characteristics of burnout in yourself—a sense of inefficacy, emotional exhaustion, and cynicism?
- What are your personal emotional, physical, mental, and behavioural signs that you're starting to burn out?

Vicarious Trauma

As with burnout, most psychologists feel ill-prepared to deal with trauma, let alone the way that exposure to experiences of trauma can change us.[16] Experiencing trauma from exposure to the trauma of others is called vicarious trauma, or VT. As I have described in previous work, "Vicarious trauma can occur when you have been exposed to stories so difficult or disturbing that you, too, are traumatized by the images and details…The trauma that they [the client] experienced is 'transferred' over to you, so that you also feel the effects."[17]

Trauma does not describe an event or series of events but our nervous system's response to threatening events. From a somatic-experiencing perspective, trauma is what happens inside of us when an event occurs that is too much, too fast, or too soon for our nervous system to handle.[18] The triggering "event" could be one or more acute or prolonged experiences that involve real or perceived threats and that activate a person's survival responses: the commonly known fight, flight, and freeze responses, as well as more recently researched and understood defensive adaptations such as attach/cry-for-help, collapse/submit, and please/appease.[19]

At the nervous-system level, the body responds to experiences of direct and indirect threat in very similar ways. At an embodied level, then, vicarious trauma is just as real as direct trauma, and like direct trauma, it tends to affect our whole system—not just our body and our emotions, but also how we see ourselves and the world. In her *Compassion Fatigue Workbook*, Françoise Mathieu describes VT as a "profound shift that workers [i.e., therapists] experience in their world view when they work with clients who have experienced trauma."[20] Through this process, our sense of safety and trust in the world along with our beliefs about humanity may be fundamentally altered. Some therapists working with a high case load of intimate partner violence, for example, have reported feeling more suspicious of others and losing trust that there are good people in the world.[21]

Individual, systemic, and workplace factors all contribute to the unique ways in which each of us responds to exposure to traumatic events. These factors may also make us more or less susceptible to traumatization, including vicarious traumatization.[22] For the purposes of this book, I want to highlight what I believe is the most salient risk factor, especially for therapists: encounters with traumatic material. This type of exposure to indirect threat (e.g., hearing or reading about clients' experiences of traumatic events) is commonplace in counselling professions, making vicarious trauma a particular risk of these professions. The very nature of our roles as therapists makes us more likely to experience it.

Identifying Vicarious Trauma

Vicarious trauma is trauma, and it can be identified with the same tools we use to identify trauma in clients. A comprehensive list of PTSD assessment tools, including both clinician-administered interviews and self-report measures, can be found on the American Psychological Association website (apa.org/ptsd-guideline/assessment).

As with any measure, keep limitations in mind when working with diverse populations. For example, measures for PTSD often fail to capture the fundamental aspects of race-based trauma: that it is cumulative and systemic, rather than the result of an acute incident. When working with racial trauma, consider using instruments that are specifically designed to measure it, such as the Race-Based Traumatic-Stress Symptom Scale (RBTSSS) and the UConn Racial/Ethnic Stress and Trauma Scale (UnRESTS).[23]

To keep ourselves safe, we need to think about ways we can limit our exposure to traumatic material to make this exposure manageable, whatever that means for each of us. This is where boundaries come in. Examples of boundaries for trauma workers include limiting the number of trauma clients you see per week, reducing the total number of clients you see per day, balancing client work with other work-related tasks (e.g., supervision, teaching, or writing), or taking sufficient breaks to reset your nervous system between sessions—I try to aim for at least fifteen minutes. Boundaries outside of work are also important for avoiding vicarious trauma. You might, for example, need to more purposefully schedule time for connection and joy each day in order to help counter the risk of VT.

Reflect and Journal

- Do you recognize any of the signs of VT in yourself?
- If yes, how have you coped with them thus far? How would you like to see yourself coping?

Resentment

Boundaries are also key to avoiding resentment in our work. One definition of resentment—and, I think, a good one—is "bitter indignation at having been treated unfairly."[24] Resentment crops up when others treat us unfairly or ask too much of us—for example, if an employer asks us for more hours of work than we're able to provide, or if we aren't receiving a fair wage for our work, or if we have been denied a promotion we feel we deserve. Sometimes, specific client behaviours may bring up feelings of resentment, depending on what our own wounds are.

Interestingly, it is also common to feel resentment when we treat *ourselves* unfairly or ask *ourselves* for more than we are really willing to give. For example, many therapists end up working longer hours and taking on more tasks or clients at work than is sustainable for them, even though no one has specifically asked them to do so. This is often linked to societal pressures around productivity and constant doing (something we'll discuss in chapter 4), and around selfless, unbounded helping (as we discussed in chapter 1). When we internalize these pressures, we become one of the people making excessive demands on our own time and energy, making it that much harder to set the boundaries that even we know we need.

If you notice you are already feeling resentful in some aspect of your work, it's likely a clue that your limits have been crossed and it may be time to set a boundary. If you are not being paid fairly and it's affecting your sense of worthiness, that may mean it's time to look for another workplace or, if you can, to let go of contracts that are overtaxing you. If you are feeling resentful with a client for missing appointments, it may be time to set up a clear cancellation policy that you can abide by. If you find you've been treating yourself unfairly, consider offering yourself the same kind treatment you would offer a colleague.

> ## Reflect and Journal
> - Are you already feeling the effects of resentment? If so, how is it impacting your sense of self, and your work?
> - What are you unable to do when you're constantly saying yes to what you don't want?
> - What would you like to do that you're not currently making time and allowing energy for?

Boundaries Sustain Us

Along with avoiding burnout, VT, resentment, and the health issues they bring, people are really moved to set boundaries because they have a vision of a better life. By protecting us from occupational hazards, our boundaries protect the parts of our existence that give us life, energy, and joy. They thus protect our willingness and ability to do the work we love and to remain open and curious: they sustain us as therapists. When we set boundaries and reduce budding resentment, we make space for real connection with our clients, ourselves, and the people we love. At work, we are able to see the person in front of us with warmth and appreciation rather than irritability and cynicism. Outside work, we can begin to see the people we're in relationship with as whole and good rather than focusing on their faults and imperfections. Real connection also happens because, by setting boundaries and making our preferences known, we allow ourselves to be seen.

I believe the cornerstone to a more sustainable, fulfilling life as a therapist involves giving ourselves permission to be human, permission to have needs of our own, and permission to fulfil those needs unapologetically. Sonya Renee Taylor and adrienne maree brown understand this permission-giving process as an act of liberation and a practice we need to continually come back to: "The act of giving yourself permission is an ever-evolving process. Each day a new area of awareness may arise where you are given the opportunity to expand into even greater permission and power than the day before."[25] As we will explore through the rest of this book, the practice of setting boundaries that will sustain you in your work involves becoming curious about yourself, your needs and limits, your wants and desires, your yeses and nos, and how all of these change over time.

First-Person Perspectives

Setting boundaries for myself has become a critical part of how I work as I often worry about the repercussions of not having appropriate boundaries. In my life, I have experienced poverty and scarcity. As a result, my ability to work is very deeply connected to me feeling safe and grounded. This experience has forced me to set strong personal boundaries in the workplace as they are tied to me feeling like I can care for myself both economically and emotionally.

Running my own private practice allows me to set boundaries in line with my personal needs as a human being that also feel meaningful to how I approach my work. For example, I can choose when it makes sense to work more and when it makes sense to cut back. It has also allowed me to practice in a way where I can address systemic inequities without fear of retribution from an employer.

It has taken me several years to come to this conclusion and I still find it difficult to set boundaries in work settings at times. However, this is my aspiration as I continue to grow in my career as a therapist.

—*Melody Cesar, MSW, RSW*

It's important to find ways to "stay fit" for practice: good trainers/training, good personal self-care (or, as I like to call it, "nervous-system management," to give it more importance), and sufficient periods of rest to recover and come back to oneself. I have burnt out on more than one occasion, and often it's because I was failing to take into account how demanding this work is and trying to just keep going at my usual pace, despite changing circumstances in other areas of life and needing more space to process and adjust.

—*Andrea, Registered Psychologist*

When Is It Time to Set Boundaries?

In an ideal world, we would all be ready to set boundaries before we start losing track of the joy that sustains us, and well before we experience burnout, VT, and resentment. But if you're already experiencing burnout, VT, or resentment—or any combination of these—know that you're not alone, and that it's certainly not too late to start setting boundaries and finding your way back to what sustains you. The more we practice boundaries, the earlier we'll be able to address the factors that lead to occupational harms, and the less likely it will be that they interfere with our quality of life and our ability to continue in this profession.

But this is not a perfect process, and we will all make mistakes along the way. Many therapists make the mistake of sticking with a work situation longer than what's good for their health and well-being because they feel that they "should." As Nedra Tawwab, licensed therapist and author of *Set Boundaries, Find Peace*, reminds us, "Sometimes it's best to leave before you reach your breaking point. It's okay to pivot without suffering for a prolonged period. Staying until you can't take anymore takes a lot out of you. Enough can be enough at your discretion."[26] When you find yourself in a difficult work environment, ask yourself: If nothing were to change in my current situation, how long could I persist in it without it being a detriment to my physical or mental health? Just because you are technically able to get through another week in a certain environment doesn't mean that you "should."

There is no single, objective point at which a situation becomes too much for someone. We all have our own breaking points. When and how we reach those points is absolutely individual and influenced by a multitude of factors, including how overloaded we're already feeling in the rest of our lives, our level of experience in the work we're doing, the supports we have in place, our previous life experiences, and the particular societal pressures we feel. What burns you out might not burn out your co-worker. What causes them resentment may be something you're okay with doing. We all have to find our own limits, and when we find that we've reached those limits, we may well feel that something needs to change.

First-Person Perspectives

Knowing when to set a new boundary is primarily a body feeling for me. My boundaries have changed throughout my life based on what is happening for my physical self, as well as what is happening in my life outside of work, so it's something I have to keep listening to.

—Claire Wilde, MEd, RPsych, CST

I've noticed behavioural and situational indicators that let me know it's time to set a boundary: when I am struggling to be assertive with time, when my sessions run longer than scheduled, and when I find I spend more time on out-of-session communication with the client.

There are also emotional indicators: when I feel impatient with my clients; when I notice the urge to provide a solution to their problem (versus guiding them through it); when I notice anger or frustration when a client is not showing progress (i.e., when my expectations override the natural pace of a client's healing process); when I struggle to maintain clinical objectivity and notice biases influencing my ability to be nonjudgmentally present for my clients; when I don't feel (at least a little bit) excited to go to work; and when I notice an internal sense of relief in response to a short-notice cancellation.

—Olga Yakovlyeva, Registered Psychologist

I usually know it's time to revisit or set a personal boundary when I begin to feel disconnected from my work. This can look like resenting the work or feeling like there is no purpose in what I am doing.

— Melody Cesar, MSW, RSW

It becomes clear to me that I need to set a boundary when I am feeling the early signs of burnout, especially resentment, or if I am thinking excessively about clients or work matters outside of my usual office hours. Both of those are clear indicators of a need to shift and reconsider my boundaries.

—Susan Larcombe, Registered Psychologist

It is important, however, to start setting boundaries only when you're ready to do so. That means being ready to communicate those boundaries with others, to act on them when you need to, and to change them when they no longer reflect your needs. Often, people set sweeping, rigid boundaries early before they're ready to act on them—perhaps because a well-meaning friend or therapist has told them it's time to set a boundary, or because they're really hoping that by doing so, other people will finally understand what they need and behave accordingly. Then, when a colleague, supervisor, or client doesn't react to their boundary in the way that they were hoping, they find themselves sliding back into old patterns of putting other people's needs before their own. Remember: If you aren't ready to respect your own boundaries and act in ways that reflect your needs, your boundaries are unlikely to be effective.

Setting boundaries when you're ready also means setting them on your own timeline and not because someone else told you that you "should." Sometimes we know that a situation isn't working for us, that we're in a toxic environment, that a change needs to occur—and sometimes we also know that we're not quite ready to make a change. It's okay not to be ready. It's okay to take your time. Boundary-setting is a process, and as healing as it is, it's not always straightforward. Still, you can breathe easy. As you learn about boundaries and consider making changes, know that you don't need to jump into action. You don't need to do anything differently just yet. Allow yourself the time and space that you need; moving at your own pace is what will support your growth.

Of course, none of us want to stick with an untenable situation indefinitely. Work at your own pace, but do begin: Turn toward your head, heart, and body, and find out what decision is right for you today.

Boundary Practice

Reflect on the following questions and make a note of your answers. Refer back to your answers frequently as you work through this book. When you do, ask yourself: Do my answers still ring true? If not, allow yourself to change or adjust them to better align with your changing needs and perspectives.

- How will I show up for myself with compassion and integrity when I make mistakes?
- How can I continue to align myself with my values when others are disappointed by my actions?
- Who can I trust to see the best in me, especially when it's hard for me to see it?

3

Boundaries as Embodied Decisions

One of the first steps in setting boundaries is understanding your own limits. Understanding your limits involves paying attention not just to what you *think* those limits are, but also to how you feel, in your emotions and your body, in different situations.

The Anatomy of Embodied Decisions

Setting boundaries that truly respect our needs involves listening to the information we receive from three sources of knowledge in our embodied selves—our heads, hearts, and bodies—and using it in an integrated way to better understand where we are, where we are going, what we need, and what boundaries to set in order to respond to those needs. I call this process *embodied decision-making*. Let's break down the three sources of knowledge in an embodied decision part by part.

The head represents your thoughts and cognition. It is the part of you that connects with reason and is driven by your frontal lobe. The head can help you to evaluate pros and cons to a particular course of action, and it can help you look at evidence about how similar situations have been for you in the past. Perhaps you previously struggled in a private practice where you were expected to take on most of the administrative work yourself, or you found yourself overwhelmed when you didn't have enough time to unwind between clients. These are good cues about how you will respond to similar situations in the future, and are worth looking back on if you find yourself facing one of these situations again. Your head can also help you remember what works for you: the type of supervisor or manager you need, for instance, or the client issues you work best with.

The heart represents your emotion centre. It connects you to your feelings about a situation or person. Usually, these feelings can be given names: happiness, calm, joy, fear, sadness, anger, and so on. The emotions we notice can help us understand what it's like for us to be in different situations, and how we're doing overall. Think, for example, of a client you struggle with or a challenge in your workplace and notice the emotions that arise. Do you feel anxious and irritable with that person or in that environment? Do you feel calm and grounded? When reflecting on your life as a whole, you can ask yourself if you regularly feel drained and depleted or connected and satisfied. Your emotions can also be used as a gauge: How would you feel if you made *this* decision? What about *that* one?

The body is the third piece in the embodied-self triad. It represents all your physical sensations and connects you to your so-called gut feelings or intuition, as well as to the way your body holds the story of what you're experiencing. A tightness in the stomach or a heaviness in your chest can say a lot. Consistent headaches and gastrointestinal issues are also good cues to pay attention to. Frequently getting sick or feeling overly exhausted are other signs. Physical pain issues that don't resolve with treatment may be an expression of a deeper pain being held within.

Reflect and Journal

Think of a challenge you are dealing with at work or have dealt with at work. How have you been approaching it so far, or how did you deal with it? Ask yourself some questions to gather information from your head, heart, and body. For smaller challenges, the cognitive, emotional, and physical cues may be subtler than what we're used to noticing, so I invite you to really get curious, and see if you can attune to what's happening inside you. What are you aware of? Take a few minutes to jot down what your head, heart, and body have to say.

Head: What are the benefits and drawbacks of approaching this challenge in the way that I am? Does what I'm doing fit my values?

Heart: Does this feel right to me? Do I like the situation I'm in? What other emotions are arising?

Body: What does my body want to do? Am I safe from harm?

Listening to Your Body

Sometimes we get stuck because we're used to prioritizing one part of ourselves over others. For many people in Western culture, it's our heads. If that sounds like you, it's important to acknowledge it and to understand that it is not the only way to position yourself. Yes, we *do* need to listen to our heads, but if we say yes to a client or employer request based on cognition alone ("This should be fine" or "I technically have time"), we risk ignoring important clues from the rest of our selves. As trauma therapist Jordan Pickell writes, "Emotions are ancestral tools that can tell us when our boundaries have been crossed and when it is time to take action. If you are stifling your irritation and resentment, if you are saying yes with clenched fists, you are squashing the exact emotions and body sensations that are there to give you direction."[1] Remind yourself in the same way you'd remind your clients that no emotion or bodily sensation is "bad." Your body will tell you what nourishes you and what depletes you. Whatever arises inside is there to alert you of something, even if you don't understand it at first.

Of the three parts of the embodied-self triad, the body—our physical sensations—tend to be the most often ignored. I encourage therapists to pay special attention to their bodies, as they convey important information that cannot be found in our heads or hearts. One of the biggest invitations you will hear from me is to practice listening to the wisdom of your body. When we listen inward, we can attend to the information our bodies give us and start thinking about our needs. This may look like taking the first signs of a headache as a cue to slow down, ground yourself, and put away the to-do list. It might involve recognizing the tightness in your jaw as a deeper representation of your healthy anger that tells you you're not okay with something that just happened. We learn to ignore our bodies in favour of our heads in so many ways, and confronting these lessons is important to moving past them and coming back to our whole selves.

In *The Body Is Not an Apology*, Sonya Renee Taylor writes about the lessons North American society teaches about bodies. From an early age, we are taught to view our bodies as something to overcome or to fix. We are methodologically disconnected from our bodies and taught to see them through a lens of shame. Taylor points out that these lessons have a purpose: they are profitable for those in power. "Body shame," she says, "flourishes in our world because profit and power depend on it."[2] I appreciate how Taylor straightforwardly reminds us that we feel the way we do because of real forces and events in the world and in our lives. No amount of simply thinking differently will fix the structural inequities, traumas, and injustices that are the root cause of our suffering (something we'll explore more in chapter 4).

Psychology has long been run from a standpoint of prioritizing reason as a method of overcoming the suffering we experience in our bodies and through our emotions. If we are truly going to invite clients to let go of shame and listen to their bodies, however, we must also learn to come home to our whole, embodied selves. This practice is in line with a decolonized or Indigenized approach to therapy. Know, however, that this process can be unfamiliar, uncomfortable, or even downright distressing.

Reflect and Journal
- How has being disconnected from your body (or feeling ashamed of it) thwarted you?
- How has disconnection helped you survive?

Disconnection, whether from ourselves or others, is often a survival strategy, so starting to reconnect may feel dangerous or threatening. I encourage you to take this practice slowly and with support if you need it.

As you begin to practice listening to your body, try naming the sensations that come up. Many people are more familiar with and attuned to painful bodily sensations than pleasant ones, which makes sense: It's in our body's best interest to alert us when something is uncomfortable or painful so that we can deal with it. Tuning into our painful physical sensations is important to understanding our "no." As we know, however, boundaries are also about finding our "yes," so while you practice listening to your body, try connecting with and naming your (often less obvious) pleasant sensations as well. If naming body sensations is new to you, it may help to have a list of possible descriptions. Here are some of my favourites:

- Heavy
- Light
- Tight
- Knotted
- Open
- Flowing

- Buzzy
- Numb
- Energized
- Warm
- Expanded
- Spacious

When my clients are first starting to reconnect with their body's pleasant feelings, they will often say things like "It feels *less* tense" or "I *don't* feel as tight." They define their pleasant bodily sensations in the negative; they have a hard time naming more comfortable or enjoyable sensations except by relating them to the absence of painful ones. If that rings true for you, I challenge you, when you next experience a pleasant sensation, to notice not only what it *isn't*, but what it *is*. Do you feel ease, or presence, or relaxation? Do you feel warm, or energetic, or lazy?

Pleasant, unpleasant, and even neutral, the more you practice naming and acknowledging the range of sensations you experience in your body—by expanding your vocabulary for physical sensations beyond just "bad" and "not so bad"—the more adept you'll be at knowing where you stand on situations in your life and work, and what you need moving forward.

Exercise: Making an Embodied Decision

Understanding the different sources of information that go into embodied decision-making is a necessary first step. But how do you use this information to actually make an embodied decision—that is, to set a boundary? Use the template below to work through the process for yourself.

First, think of an upcoming work-related decision (big or small) that you need to make. Next, list your options. At this point you don't need to judge the options—just write them out. For each option listed, I invite you to connect with your head, heart, and body and to mindfully check in with what they have to offer to your understanding about where your whole, embodied self stands, and what you really want. Write out how your head, heart, and body respond to each option, then take a step back. Does anything stand out to you as a definite embodied yes or no? Do you notice any conflicts?

I have to decide about: _____

Option 1:	Option 2	Option 3
My head says...	My head says....	My head says....
My heart says...	My heart says....	My heart says....
My body says...	My body says....	My body says...

When Parts of You Conflict

It's rare that we look inside and find our head, heart, and body in complete alignment. Once you're more comfortable listening to all three aspects of yourself, you'll likely begin to notice that, while these aspects all have important information to contribute to your understanding of your limits, they don't always agree. This is normal, but it can make embodied decision-making especially tricky. When we notice that parts of ourselves are in conflict, it's a good cue to slow down and listen.

Conflict, including inner conflict, is challenging for many people. In my work as a clinician and supervisor of other clinicians, I've noticed that many people—clients and supervisees alike—prefer to handle inner conflicts by ignoring them. They do this either by attempting to altogether avoid making a decision that would resolve the conflict or by allowing one dominant part of themselves to make the decision without input from the other parts. When we notice that we have a pattern of favouring one part of ourselves over others, it might be time to ask for outside help, either from a trusted friend or a hired expert. Even when we know we are biased toward one part of ourselves, the habit can be difficult to overcome on our own. A trusted outside eye can help us watch for our biases, identify when they are getting in the way of listening to our whole selves, and begin learning to listen to the parts of ourselves that we haven't historically prioritized. If you do decide to seek help, choose your outside observer carefully. The process of learning to fully listen to ourselves can be hindered by those around us who haven't done their own work, and who themselves uncritically prioritize one part of themselves—and therefore of you—over others.

There is an important distinction to make here between leaning on outside help to learn to listen to *ourselves* versus prioritizing the opinions of an outside observer over our own. Many of us in Western society are already well versed in placing other people's opinions and values above our own and trying to use outside perspectives as rulebooks for our own lives. This can cause us to lose touch with what really nourishes us and to feel immobilized or unable to choose a path forward. The point of seeking outside help to address a bias within ourselves is not to learn to distrust the part of ourselves that we are biased toward. It is to learn to trust *more* parts of ourselves and allow them all to contribute to our decisions. Listening to ourselves fully—head, heart, and body—is a wonderful foundation for reconnection with our personal needs, desires, and values.

Reflect and Journal

Can you think of a time your head, heart, and body have been in conflict? I invite you to revisit one of those times and work through it from the whole-body decision-making perspective. What did the different parts of yourself have to say about that situation and the different options you had in front of you? What were the points on which your head, heart, and body conflicted? How did you approach or address those conflicts? What, if anything, did you ultimately decide to do? There are no right or wrong answers here—what we do may vary greatly based on our values, our culture, our stage in life, the other circumstances surrounding the scenario, our past experiences and feelings of safety, and so much more. The task here is not to judge whether you took the right or wrong course of action, but simply to get curious about how you have handled inner conflict in the past, and how you might like to handle it going forward.

Reflect and Journal

Can you think of people in your life who you can trust to help you look at your situation in a non-judgmental way?

Anxiety, Fear, and "Wrong" Decisions

On our paths of learning there will be challenges. One very common challenge when dealing with inner conflict is anxiety. When I talk with people about learning to listen to their whole selves, I hear a lot of questions about fear and anxiety. How can we know when a feeling of fear or anxiety is protecting us from a real danger or telling us about a real value or need we have in a particular situation? And how can we know when it's connected to an old fear that doesn't really have a place in the decision we're trying to make and that is getting in the way of something we'd actually like to do?

Let's say you've been working with clients one-on-one for a number of years and are now trying to decide if you should agree to facilitate a new drop-in therapy group. It would be normal to feel nervous in this situation. It would also be normal to work through other considerations. Maybe you're questioning whether the timing works for you, whether your style would be a good fit for the group, or whether you'd be able to work with so many people at once. Maybe you've also been looking to try something new at work or are interested in what it would be like to work in a group setting. Maybe you've even had a goal of facilitating a therapy group, and this is your first opportunity to reach that goal. And maybe you also feel you need to say yes to this opportunity to keep growing in your career. You feel that familiar twist in your gut: You're anxious about having to make this decision, but you aren't exactly sure why, and you aren't exactly sure what your next move should be.

When you feel that twist, that physical sensation, in any situation, I invite you to notice it, name it, do you best to listen to the other parts of yourself (head and heart), and then make your *best guess* at what the right decision will be going forward.

"Okay," I sometimes hear, "but what about when you listen to yourself, evaluate everything, and then make the wrong decision?" In this question, I hear another: "What if I make a decision that felt like the right decision in the moment but feels like the wrong decision later on?" These are important questions to ask, and ones that many of us have. I believe answering them involves remembering an important step: You are able to react to what comes next. After you make your best guess about the right decision for you, *pay attention to how that decision is for you*, in your head, heart, and body, as you live it out. Then, if you need to, re-evaluate.

In our example, let's say you decide, based on your best guess, to facilitate the group. The experience of making the decision is going to give you more information about your limits and what you can and cannot tolerate. As the start of the group approaches, you sit with the decision and listen. Maybe you learn that the initial twist in your gut is a manageable feeling of anxiety about undertaking a new role, and that you end up feeling better once you begin the group. You might learn that the anxiety of working through certain aspects of your struggle is too overwhelming right now, and that you need to slow down, ask for a cofacilitator who has more experience, and find some support of your own. Or you might learn that the twist in your gut was telling you that this group is not the right fit for you, that your initial intuition was leading you away from it, and that you need to step back from it. In other words, your initial decision—"Yes, I'll facilitate this group"—will produce more information and lead to other decisions, whether that's a reiteration of your initial "yes," a "yes, but also," or even a "no." Some decisions will be clear while others will be more difficult to discern. When we're faced with difficult decisions, it is difficult to feel confident in advance about which path to take, but we can learn to make better guesses with some practice, patience, and a willingness to take the risk and make a decision in the first place.

Part of that practice will be learning to distinguish between challenges that are good for us to undertake—that gut twist that goes away once we begin—and those that might be too much or too overwhelming for us right now. Good challenges involve growth, so you might imagine a gentle stretch of your boundaries that slowly expands them over time. It's uncomfortable, but not outside your window of tolerance. If you try to push your boundaries too far too quickly, they'll snap you back to the where you began (and maybe even a little further) like an elastic band. During overwhelming situations, you experience a physiological stress response in which your body receives a huge dose of adrenaline and your survival instincts take over. When your survival instincts are engaged, the only thing your system is tuned into is the perceived danger and how to best avoid or brace for it. These instincts are important and valuable—they are there to keep you safe when you're in danger—but they do not allow you to be open to learning or growth. When a decision causes you so much stress that your body takes over and you feel that you're in danger, it's a good cue that it's probably not the right decision for you at this time, and it may be time to take a step back into a space where you *are* able to learn and grow.

When we do make a decision that we later realize was not the right one for us, these "wrong decisions" are not failures of decision-making. They are opportunities to learn something new about ourselves and our limits, and that is not failing. Recognizing when a path we've taken isn't quite right for us allows us to better discern what we want to do the next time around. With patience and practice, we get better at discerning "I'm nervous but I want to do this" from "I don't feel like doing this in this way, but I would be okay doing it in a different way" from "I don't feel like doing this because I don't feel safe right now."

The idea of trying something out and learning from your experience is called *reality testing*. In the process of understanding your limits, you'll do your best to make decisions based on what feels right, and sometimes you're going to make mistakes. Like everyone else, you'll make mistakes about what you think you can handle, like taking on too many volunteer hours on top of your paid work, or not giving yourself enough time in between a four-day training and your next day of client work. You will also make mistakes because you have imperfect or incomplete information, like taking on a job that sounded like a good fit on paper but didn't align with your values in practice, or realizing that a project is more complex than how it was originally described to you, or learning only after seeing a client for a length of time that they are struggling with an issue outside your scope.

It's a trap to look back at these situations and beat yourself up for making the "wrong" decision. We all make the best decisions we can at the time based on the information available to us, and that's the best we can do. It sometimes results in heartache and disappointment, but you are not alone in those feelings. They are a difficult yet essential part of figuring out who we are in this world.

Embodied Decisions About Self-Care

Embodied decision-making also applies to decisions about self-care. Say you signed up for a professional-development training. When you first signed up, it was exciting, it felt like something that would really help your practice, and you were full of energy to engage in it. As the day gets closer, however, you realize sixteen hours of your rare, sunny weekend will be eaten up by sitting inside at the training, or that the training falls at the end of an especially busy week and you feel you could really use a day or two to sleep in. We all encounter these difficult scenarios where it really is tough to know what's best for us: leisure? relaxation? professional development? Tune inward and listen to what your whole, embodied self has to say. Does anything stand out as the right decision in your whole self? What about in each part—your head, heart, and body? Remember that you are allowed to make a decision, then change your mind. You're also allowed to modify a decision to fit your needs. If, in our example, you're really not sure what to do about the training session because parts of you are in conflict—your body and heart want some free time on the weekend but your head doesn't want to miss the training altogether—you can always show up for the first half of the training and then head home. Yep: You can make a decision to honour *both* of your desires. Many people I work with are taken aback to realize this is a real possibility, so I'll highlight this again: It doesn't have to be all or nothing. It's okay to do some but not all.

This idea can be applied in a number of different ways, both at work and at home. You could take on a project and give it 80 percent effort. You could collaborate on projects instead of doing them alone. When you're trying to rejuvenate outside work, you could do ten minutes of art at home instead of a whole class. You could walk around the block if you're not sure you're up for an entire run. This isn't rude or lazy. It's about being self-sufficient, knowing where your limits are, and allowing yourself to see the continuum of possibilities. It helps us get past the pass-or-fail framework and the please-or-disappointment dichotomy.

> ## Reflect and Journal
>
> - Reflect on a recent work-related situation in which you listened to yourself fully and were glad you did.
> - Look to the week ahead. If you were to make an embodied decisions about self-care this week, what would it look like?

Accepting Your Whole, Embodied Self

In an old episode of *Dear Sugar*, host and memoirist Cheryl Strayed shared insights about learning to listen to herself that have stuck with me: Honouring what you hear when you listen to yourself is not a one-time event; it's a practice and an ongoing process. "This is not something you learn one time or do one time," Strayed said. "It's something you do every day, over and over again, for years and years and years."[3] Strayed and co-host Steve Almond's interviewee on this episode, singer India Arie, added that the practice of self-listening is a kind of leap of faith toward oneself: "I feel like people who are thoughtful…will find the impetus to take the leap, because you realize that there's a truth there that you want to honor more than you want to honor not making other people in your life mad."[4] That truth, I think, is embodied in the answers we hear when we listen inward to our whole selves.

As you practice listening to yourself, you need to practice being open to hearing the answers that your head, heart, and body are giving. This in itself can be challenging, especially when those answers conflict either with each other or with expectations we feel from outside. Referring a client out, turning down a job opportunity, or asking for what we need in our jobs is a brave and scary thing, especially when we're not sure it's the right decision.

It can be just as scary when our boss, our colleagues, external factors, or some old fear from long ago tell us that it's the wrong decision even when we know, in our whole selves, that it's right. Practice helps us honour our embodied decisions, but it doesn't "make perfect," and that's okay. Every decision is an opportunity to learn.

Boundary Practice

Use the embodied decision-making exercise above to make a work-related decision. Start small and give yourself room to play. Notice the results: How was your experience?

4

Barriers to Boundaries

The Struggle Is Real

Struggling to understand our needs and set boundaries is normal. For most people, boundary-setting doesn't come automatically. It takes practice and courage to learn to listen to ourselves and honour our needs, desires, and limits. On top of this, there are real external and material barriers that can get in our way.

Feminist approaches to counselling remind us that context is important to understanding the truth of any situation. In this chapter, I want to offer some context for the struggle many people, including therapists, have around setting boundaries. The pervasiveness of this struggle suggests that the reasons for it lie not with individual people but with social and environmental contexts that we share, both as a society and at a smaller scale. My goal is to get curious about this struggle and about the societal factors— the social injustices, the material needs, and the societal expectations, for examples—that contribute to it, and that are outside of our personal control. Understanding these factors will, I hope, help you approach your own boundary struggles with compassion.

I also encourage you to get curious about factors beyond your control that are more specific to your own life—the family context in which you grew up, for example, and the one that immediately surrounds you now. Self-reflective practices like this are vital to therapists as they help us understand and challenge what we take with us into the therapy room. These same self-reflective practices can help us better choose how we want to organize our own lives.

Societal Messages

Most helping professionals I've talked to struggle with boundaries. To me, it's no wonder. We exist in a world that has taught us to prioritize productivity over health, doing over being, and other people's comfort over our own peace of mind. We receive these messages both directly and indirectly, and they influence all of us, even if we have cultivated a critical awareness of them, because of their ubiquity—they are, to a greater or lesser extent for each of us, part of the societal "air" we breathe.

Productivity over Health

Many clients and therapists I work with report feeling that they need to earn their rest and leisure time, whether through accomplishments, acts of service, or some other unnamed standard of productivity. Unfortunately, the push toward productivity affects our personal, emotional, and physical well-being—a fact that has implications for our ability to connect with others, and therefore our ability to do our work as therapists. Agreeing to take on more work automatically means less time for taking care of our own needs. Many people struggle to allow their bodies the rest and recuperation they need, often pushing beyond reasonable limits in the name of productivity. It's common to work through our lunch breaks, cut our sleep short, cancel quality time with friends and family, and ignore even our basic needs so that we can "get things done." Many people will also delay going for regular check-ups with their medical practitioners because it may involve taking time off work. We tend to be unwilling to give up our to-do list unless our body absolutely forces us to stop.

Three of the most common physical needs we forgo in the name of productivity are eating, sleeping, and going to the bathroom. It's so easy to shrug these things off as no big deal, but they can have serious consequences in both the immediate and long term. Skipping meals destabilizes our blood sugar levels, which can impact our mood and our ability to concentrate. Meta-analysis of observational studies has shown a significant relationship between skipping breakfast and increased depression, stress, and psychological distress.[1] Skipping breakfast is also associated with increased risk of death from cardiovascular disease.[2]

The impacts of not going to the bathroom can also have serious effects. Holding urine can weaken the bladder muscles over time, which can eventually lead to incontinence or to not being able to fully empty the bladder. It can also cause urinary tract infections because bacteria can build up in the urethra when it isn't regularly flushed out. In more serious cases, regularly holding urine for extended periods can increase our risk of kidney disease. Holding in bowel movements can also have negative long-term consequences, including constipation and impactions, which may require laxatives or, in severe instances, surgery to treat.[3]

The effects of regular sleep deprivation can be equally alarming. In the short term, it can cause problems with attention, problem-solving, creativity, and reaction times. Drowsiness also puts people at higher risks for car accidents and accidents at work.[4] If that doesn't convince you of the importance of sleep, here's one final consideration to drive it home: In the famous Whitehall II Study, researchers looked at how sleep patterns affected the mortality of more than 10,000 British civil servants. The results showed that a decrease in sleep duration over the long term significantly increased study participants' risk of death from all causes, and in particular from cardiovascular disease.[5] The push to always be productive puts a huge amount of stress on our bodies. Remember the stress-response cycle we discussed in chapter 3: The initial dump of adrenaline and cortisol that we get when dealing with an acute stressor is designed to help us fight, run away, or otherwise deal with an immediate, short-lived threat. However, a chronic state of stress and the high level of cortisol that go with it have a negative impact on our health, particularly our immune system.[6]

Yet when we *do* try to stop or slow down to take care of our needs, we end up having to fight for our right to do so. First and foremost, we have to battle the inevitable guilt that comes from *not* "hanging in there" and, in some cases, shameful messages from others ("You're not doing enough," "Who do you think you are?"). We also have to battle the real barriers around us that make slowing down and listening to our own internal guidance a difficult undertaking. For students, there is pressure to publish, to graduate, to secure grant funding, and sometimes to follow bad advice from a supervisor. For clinicians, there is pressure to fill our schedules, get ahead financially, and take on any client who reaches out.

Both the value we place on productivity and the negative consequences we experience for taking the rest we need contribute to situations of burnout and difficulty setting boundaries. I've worked with many people who were passed over for promotions because, by taking sick days and trying to bring in an element of balance, they were seen

Reflect and Journal

- Were you taught (directly or indirectly) to ignore what doesn't feel good to you in the name of productivity? In what ways?
- Are there ways in which you have internalized the idea that productivity is more important than your health? If so, in what ways?

as "not being a team player," "lazy," or "not caring enough." When taking care of yourself has an impact on your job security and financial health, of course people struggle with setting boundaries and scaling back.

Doing over Being

When we're constantly having to recover from situations and events that stress our bodies and negatively impact our health, we end up being less productive than we would be if we proactively engaged in practices that support our well-being. A more sustainable approach—one that supports both our "being" and our "doing"—is clearly needed. And yet it can be hard to practice what we know to be true, especially for those of us in whom productivity is so ingrained. Many people express the pressures of productivity by constantly doing.[7] We feel compelled to keep busy, keep productive, and keep getting things done. Omid Safi, a teacher of spirituality and professor of Islamic Studies at Duke University, has also noticed this compulsion. He asks important questions about how we ended up with so much "doing" and so little "being" in our lives:

> What happened to a world in which we can sit with the people we love so much and have slow conversations about the state of our heart and soul, conversations that slowly unfold, conversations with pregnant pauses and silences that we are in no rush to fill?

> How did we create a world in which we have more and more and more to do with less time for leisure, less time for reflection, less time for community, less time to just…be?[8]

I connect with Safi's yearning for a world where kids and adults alike get messy, get lost in dreams, and get bored. The "doing" mindset interferes with these possibilities, and even shows up in the way we talk to each other. As psychologist-turned-spiritual-leader Ram Dass and journalist Paul Gorman note in *How Can I Help?*, when we meet someone new, the first question we ask is often "What do you do?" We try to get to know people according to what jobs they take on in the world, sometimes to the point of beginning to equate who people and are with what they do—and, inevitably, who *we* are with what we do.[9] This limited point of view excludes so many facets of human being. When we focus so much on doing, we miss out on who people are. This is especially true when a person's job doesn't align with their interests and passions and when their work is largely unpaid household labour like childcare.

Conflating people's doing with their being often coincides with the belief, conscious or not, that a person's value is defined by what they do and how much of themselves they give to their work. Many of us have learned to believe this from an early age. I believe there is a real danger in not seeing people's worth outside of what they do. As culture reporter Anne Helen Petersen notes, "When one's value depends on the capacity to work…[certain people] become 'less than' in the larger societal equation."[10] Putting people into a hierarchy makes it easier to justify existing systems of discrimination and oppression.

Like physician and author Gabor Maté, I believe that we're all born worthy and whole: "No human being is 'useless', whether the helpless infant or the helpless ill or dying adult." In this statement, Maté doesn't mean to suggest that we ought to extend the category of "usefulness" to all human beings, but that we ought to stop using productivity to measure people's worth. As Maté writes, "The point is…to reject the spurious concept that people need to be useful in order to be valued."[11] Our worth has nothing to do with the things we accomplish or how much we do for someone. It only takes thinking of the people in your own life who don't have much to offer in terms of productivity but mean so much to you to drive this point home. There is so much more to life and to who we are as humans than what we can materially offer to other people. Neither you nor anyone needs to be productive to be deserving of care.

> ## Reflect and Journal
> - Do you find yourself keeping busy, filling your time, and even feeling guilty when you aren't engaged in something task-oriented?
> - What would it be like to slow down, take a breath, and just be, even for a moment? Can you try it now? Write down what you notice.

Others over Self

Many therapists have learned throughout their lives and through their professional educations that hard work, generosity, and ensuring the comfort of others are of utmost importance, even if they come at a cost to oneself. In general, putting others' needs ahead of our own is seen, in North America, as a "nice" thing to do, and niceness is valued highly. As a therapist, we are often surrounded by people who are experiencing deep suffering, and pushing through our own discomfort to help those people is one way many therapists have found to cope with this reality. Prioritizing the needs of others can even become an identity. Offering more hours than we can sustain, taking on clients that are not within our scope, or not sharing our needs with our supervisor or manager can begin to feel like not just what we do but who we are: people who push through our own needs in the service of others.

This push-through mentality tends to be celebrated in Western culture, whether a person is pushing through a physical issue like pain or sickness or an emotional one like grief or acute fear. Its valorization is materially reflected in our work infrastructure—for example, the terribly low number of days that the Government of Canada offers federally regulated employees for bereavement leave (three).[12] Stress leave is stigmatized, with many people who take it finding that they're put under scrutiny ("Are you really that sick?") and pushed out of their jobs when they do return to work by way of ostracization, re-organization, and otherwise thinly veiled attempts to make the work environment inhospitable to them. People who take stress leave are often seen as people who "just can't handle the work." The challenges that they are experiencing and the ways they try to take care of themselves are brushed off as weaknesses rather than cues to a larger workplace or even larger societal problem.

When we allow others needs to overshadow our own, it can become difficult to find the time, or even the justification, to take care of ourselves. We all have a voice inside of us that speaks when we are approaching our limits. Yet, as Emily and Amelia Nagoski point out in their book *Burnout: The Secret to Unlocking the Stress Cycle*, our social training can gives us "an extraordinary capacity to ignore this voice."[13] As Gabor Maté illustrates in his book *When the Body Says No*, ignoring this inner voice can cause us serious harm. He describes noticing a pattern in many of his patients with chronic illnesses such as multiple sclerosis, inflammatory ailments, chronic fatigue syndrome, autoimmune disorders, fibromyalgia, migraine, skin disorders, and endometriosis, among others: They tended to deal with significant stresses in their lives by pushing past the signals telling them that they'd passed their limits.[14] Maté suggests that this coping may have contributed to the onset of his patients' conditions, which is not to say that these medical conditions are the patients' fault, but that we live in a world that puts a great deal of pressure on us to ignore our stress, which can have serious and long-lasting consequences on our lives.

Being able to persevere through difficulty can be a strength; when we need to draw on this strength every day over a long period of time, however, it becomes harmful. When we are always attempting to push *through* our needs for the sake of others, we're really pushing our

Reflect and Journal

- What phrases have you heard that encourage people to not listen to themselves? Has anyone ever said these things to you?
- Have you ever felt that other people's needs are more important than yours? When? Has this feeling ever shown up in your work with clients?

own experience *down*. Eventually, the things we push down will bubble up in us in different ways. If we are to continue offering effective services as therapists, we must make ourselves a priority.

Structural Issues in Society

Our society is organized around a variety of institutions and systems that impact the ways in which we interact with one another, the opportunities we have access to, and the limitations we experience. These institutions include political and economic policies, legal systems, and business practices. Ideally, this social structure creates agreed-upon rules and norms that help us live well together, but some social structures fail to serve us as individuals or communities and have negative material impacts on our lives. This sort of structural failure is at the roots of, for example, the disproportionate numbers of BIPOC individuals in the prison system, wage disparity along lines of gender and race, and buildings and events that are inaccessible to people with disabilities.

Structural issues can make it extremely difficult to set boundaries because they affect our lives in material ways but are beyond our individual control. Let's take a closer look at a few of these issues.

Systemic Injustices and Marginalization

Most therapists encounter the messages of productivity over health, doing over being, and others over self in some way, but the impacts of these messages will look different for each of us. This is because all of our experiences are mitigated by facets of identity such as race, gender, class, and ability.

Systemic injustices occur when the social, economic, and political systems in which we live are structured in ways that prioritize certain groups over others and lead to unequal opportunities and outcomes across different demographics. Demographics that systematically experience poorer outcomes can be described as "marginalized"—that is, they are on the margins of the prioritized group. In North America, marginalized identities include women, LGBTQ+ populations, BIPOC populations, people with disabilities, and low-income people, among others. Many people hold multiple intersecting identities of marginalization, such as Black and queer or disabled and low-income. People who belong to one or more marginalized groups tend to encounter more societal barriers than those who don't.

For example, according to the 2022 *Women in the Workplace* report, women as an entire group are disproportionally exposed to microaggressions, are overworked and underpaid, and report that personal characteristics (such as gender or parenting status) have played a role in negative work experiences such as being passed over for leadership opportunities.[15] Women with other marginalized identities face further challenges. For example, LGBTQ+ women and women with disabilities report experiencing more demeaning microaggressions than other women. Women with disabilities are also significantly more likely to have their competence challenged and undermined. Latinas and Black women are less likely than other women to report feeling that their manager supports their career development.[16] Experiences like these point to structural inequities in society— beliefs, norms, and expectations that put certain groups at a disadvantage. People who are affected by structural inequities must work harder than those who are not to receive, for example, the same compensation or recognition in their jobs, exacerbating the pressures to be productive, to always do more, and to prioritize others' needs over one's own.

First-Person Perspectives

I am a biracial and queer individual from a low socioeconomic background, and this significantly impacts my ability to create and maintain boundaries. A significant part of the conversation is the power differential that is maintained against marginalized individuals, which makes it very difficult to maintain boundaries when considering our education, our work, or even our interpersonal relationships for fear of discrimination or retaliation from those in positions of power.

Additionally, growing up in a collectivist household gave me a different perspective on what boundaries I could set. I did not have the luxury of "cutting people out." People coming from a similar background may have difficulty figuring out what boundaries to set around overbearing or even abusive people in their lives. It may not be as easy as saying "Don't call me, I'll call you."

—*David, Provisionally Registered Psychologist*

The systemic injustices and marginalizations in society bleed into most professional settings in some way, including in counselling professions. Consider, for example, the barriers to entry into our profession. In most provinces, a PhD is required, along with the Examination for Professional Practice in Psychology (EPPP) and the EPPP2. This educational pathway carries a high price with limited opportunities for reliable, long-term funding and requires an extensive time commitment, making it inaccessible to people with low incomes or responsibilities such as child or family care that require the bulk of their time and income. This isn't to say that there should be less training and regulatory scrutiny in our line of work, but that, without a sustained and substantial injection of material support for students of counselling psychology, these barriers perpetuate class inequity within our profession.

After working so hard just to gain entry to the profession, marginalized therapists may have a hard time finding an accessible workplace, whether that means an office that is scent-free, has an antiracist policy, has accessible bathrooms, allows smudging and other ceremonial healing practices, permits reduced hours or a flexible work schedule, or has some other accommodation. Accessibility needs like these should be accommodated by workplaces, and in some cases accommodations may be required by law. The Alberta Human Rights Act, for example, states that employers shall not "discriminate against any person with regard to employment or any term or condition of employment because of the race, religious beliefs, colour, gender, gender identity, gender expression, physical disability, mental disability, age, ancestry, place of origin, marital status, source of income, family status or sexual orientation of that person."[17] These protected identity characteristics are called *grounds for discrimination*, or *protected grounds*. The Alberta Human Rights Commission clarifies that discrimination may be an action, policy, practice, or decision, whether intentional or unintentional, that has a negative impact on a person and is related to a protected ground.[18] Federally, employers have a legal duty to accommodate the needs of employees that are related to protected grounds as defined in the Canadian Human Rights Act.[19] Still, many people I've talked to are made to feel like a problem for outlining their accessibility needs to an employer.

Then there is the issue of therapists with marginalized identities disproportionately carrying the weight of working with marginalized clients. Anecdotally, I have spoken with therapists who feel overworked and burnt out because they are the only therapist in their community from a particular cultural group, and other therapists in the area may lack the cultural competence required to take on marginalized clients. As a result, marginalized therapists may feel an urgency to take on more than they are able to handle in terms of total caseload. This stress can be amplified when clients, themselves affected by systemic inequities, experience resource insecurity. Because marginalized therapists are so aware of the barriers to treatment faced by marginalized clients, they may feel more responsible to accept certain clients, regardless of whether doing so will stretch them beyond their limits, and regardless of their clients' ability to pay. To make it even more difficult, marginalized therapists are often celebrated for working beyond their limits to serve communities in need, which increases the pressure already on them to put others before themselves.

The solution to these problems is not simply to encourage marginalized therapists to take on fewer clients and to set boundaries for their well-being, though this is certainly part of it. But that alone will not solve the larger systemic issues that are affecting these therapists and that they are trying to address, and it will leave many clients in need without support. The whole counselling profession needs to step up and redistribute the burdens of labour that currently fall disproportionately to marginalized therapists.

First-Person Perspectives

Whether my strong work ethic was the result of immigrating to a country where my parents felt "othered" or because of the intergenerational transmission of trauma, it is hard to release the ever-present sense that I have to work harder than my white counterparts. I work harder to not be taken for granted in my workplaces; work harder to try to ensure my professional future by taking more education, training, grasping at opportunities; and work harder to "represent" my culture and my race. This last point is an existential conundrum. Theoretically, I don't want the dominant (white) culture to see me as a "credit" to my race; however, I know that, whether explicit or implicit, my achievements are measured—by white and BIPOC people alike—as exceptional.

At the same time, I am in the middle stage of my career and have witnessed the rising, unapologetic push-back on racism from persons of colour. I am beginning to challenge my own previously held beliefs about my need to comply with institutional expectations about my work.

—*Sophia C. Parks, Registered Psychologist*

I grew up as a first-gen Canadian-born child of immigrants from East Africa and Europe. From a cultural perspective, boundaries were not discussed nor are they considered part of our cultural understanding of how we present ourselves.

I have the privilege of working with other BIPOC women who have similar life experiences. I find this aspect of my work to be very fulfilling. At the same time, witnessing systemic oppression on an ongoing basis sometimes makes me feel hopeless about change. I have to create a boundary for myself when I engage in this work from a clinical perspective. I tend to balance my clinical work with larger actions aimed at dismantling systemic oppression such as advocacy, resistance, and time in community. Unfortunately, this often results in a greater demand of my emotional labour and time.

> I have come to understand that setting personal
> boundaries is a critical part of my success in my chosen
> profession. I have had to figure out how to show up in this
> way despite not always having language and understanding
> to implement boundaries at the outset.
>
> — *Melody Cesar, MSW, RSW*

Emotional Labour

Putting one's own needs aside in service of others is one definition of emotional labour. It could also be defined as the effort of managing one's own emotional responses—stuffing our true reactions down—in order to appear less emotional or needy, maintain relationships, make others feel comfortable, and ensure that things run smoothly. It is typically an unappreciated, unacknowledged, and often unpaid workload that is disproportionately borne by women and other marginalized groups.[20]

In the context of counselling work, certain therapists may feel pressure to put their needs aside to take care of the emotional lives of others, whether their clients or their colleagues. For example, marginalized employees and students are often asked to take on the labour of leading diversity, equity, and inclusion initiatives to make their workplace more equitable while at the same time dealing with the psychological impacts of working in an inequitable environment.[21] Similarly, those who work in non-profits may be expected to act as the official representative of their community on many committees on top of the job they were hired for: counselling. BIPOC therapists are more likely to be considered subject-matter experts on how to approach work with racialized people and may be approached with the additional task of providing training, offering advice, or consulting on policies or procedures without any additional time or funding to do so.[22] In the education space, I have noticed that BIPOC female instructors tend to be expected to do more emotional labour for their students and to have more lenient classroom policies than other instructors.

Women (and other people that society sees as "feminine") are often expected to take on more tasks related to support and organizing, to be pleasant in their interactions, and to never ask for or expect appreciation. When they show their own emotions in the workplace, they are frequently written off. At the same time, according to 2016 research, women are also judged more harshly for emotional restraint.[23] "Feminine" emotions are seen not as a clue to a real problem, but a mark of untrustworthiness.

One thing that stands out to me about emotional labour is that it's expected to be done without pay and, perhaps even more importantly, without acknowledgment. Writer, speaker, and former social worker Kai Cheng

Thom, speaking from her perspective as a trans woman of colour, puts it
this way:

> Instead of labor, we're taught that the work we do to care for
> others is an act of love which must be given freely, even when it
> comes at the cost of our own well-being and self-expression.
>
> We're taught to doubt ourselves, our instincts, our needs, so
> that we can play the role of loving child, friend, mother, nurse,
> therapist, lover.
>
> Women and marginalized people are taught, implicitly and
> explicitly, that part of being who we are is the paradoxical duty
> to at once understand and care for everyone else's feelings and
> desires while not having a right to our own.[24]

Knowing that emotional labour is often invisible to those who don't perform it, and even invisible to those who do, Thom uses stories from her
own life that highlight the weight of emotional labour: putting up with her
grandfather's inappropriate caresses so that she wouldn't get punished for
being "ungrateful," listening to her father discuss adult problems and holding the burden of these for him, acting as the sole emotional support and
counsellor for a friend who experienced trauma, keeping her suicidal feelings to herself because it hurt other people to hear about them, and being
expected to make her boyfriend feel better about his abusive behaviour.
It's no surprise that these early experiences of emotional labour shaped
Thom and her understanding of her worth. Now an adult, she describes
how she feels defined by others' expectations that she will be the rock-solid
caretaker, both professionally and at home. This is compounded by a fear
that if she doesn't do this caretaking, no one will. When unacknowledged
emotional labour becomes an identity, it can trap us in others-before-self
dynamics that are especially difficult to escape from.

Mothering is another area of intense emotional labour. Even in countries
that are known for gender equality, mothers continue to perform a disproportionate level of invisible, unappreciated mental and emotional work in
the home. This is exacerbated by the lack of support for mothers in the workplace.[25] Despite Canada's parental leave policies being much more extensive
than our counterparts in the United States, challenges still exist. The mental
and emotional labour of parenting doesn't disappear when parental leave
ends; that's just when a parent's other job begins again, on top of their now
under-supported, under-recognized, and usually uncompensated parenting work. According to one Canadian study, psychologist mothers who
encountered a lack of access to support from employers, coworkers, and
family members (including lack of access to childcare supports and inflex-
ibility around work hours) after returning to work decided to switch from

public to private practice so they could have greater control over how they fit their work into the rest of their lives as parents. Unfortunately, many who made this switch experienced a decrease in work-family balance, as their job responsibilities and family responsibilities began to bleed into one another.[26] As one participant described, "I felt guilty when having to take time off work to care for my children when they [were] sick. I also felt guilty for leaving on time every day."[27] The problem is not one of where we do our work, but of workload: When emotional labour is not recognized as labour, it is not counted in employers' or even our own ledgers, and this can lead to exhaustion and burnout.

In her documentary *The Mask You Live In*, Jennifer Siebel Newsom has quite powerfully explored certain kinds of emotional labour among men, as well—specifically, the way many men have been brought up to hide their softer feelings and the impacts of having to do so. In the film, educator and activist Tony Porter describes how, by the time a boy is five years old, he's been taught that it's not okay to cry in public. By ten years old, he knows exactly how to hide the hurt to conform to normative expectations that he do so. Boys aren't encouraged to talk about pain unless it's about how to solve it with violence. Dr. Judy Chu notes that these lessons teach boys a limited array of possibilities for how they can "be in the world and behave in a way that's socially acceptable. In learning to accommodate to those ideals, they're learning to conceal or just downplay qualities that are traditionally associated with girls and women."[28]

Capitalism and Financial Precarity

It's important to recognize that the pressure to be productive, selfless, and without needs of our own is not self-created. In addition to all the issues described above, living in a capitalist system means that our worth is measured by "our ability to create value for those who employ us."[29] Many of us have also been influenced by the "Protestant work ethic"—a belief system that emphasizes hard work, discipline, and frugality, and that is embedded in North American culture at large, regardless of our personal systems of faith.[30]

We now live, however, in a time of economic uncertainty in which success and financial stability is not guaranteed, even with hard work and perseverance. Those of us who grew up believing we lived in a meritocracy (a system that understands success to be based on merit rather than pre-existing social standing[31]) may find this difficult to accept. For many, it is only when our efforts fail to reap rewards that we start to question the influence of factors outside our control. Of course, many people in marginalized groups have always understood that the cards are stacked against them, because the same cards have been stacked against them for generations.

As the middle class increasingly erodes, more and more people are coming face to face with financial precarity and the realization that hard work is not a direct path to a comfortable, stable life.

The majority of psychologists practising today fall into the category of people who have had to navigate financial and job instability in a way that previous generations did not have to. Anne Helen Petersen notes that most millennials struggle to balance skyrocketing housing, childcare, and health-related costs alongside student debt. Together, these costs exceed what many full-time-employed people can afford. Regardless, the overwhelming main-stream message continues to be that all that's needed is a little more hard work. Eventually, though, most of us will look up from all of this hard work and realize: "There's no winning the system when the system itself is broken."[32]

When Barriers and Needs Conflict

Structural and personal factors outside of our control contribute to chal-lenges around boundary-setting. These challenges are especially pro-nounced for those who are marginalized. While advocating for a more just society that supports all of us is an important part of counselling profes-sions, it is not an immediate solution. In the meantime, we still need to find ways to live in this world.

Having good boundaries doesn't mean there will be no struggle, discom-fort, or conflict. It doesn't mean you will never have to do anything you'd prefer not to do, nor that the world will always deal you a fair hand, nor that you don't need to fulfil your responsibilities even when it's hard. We all have responsibilities that are probably not our favourite thing to do, whether it's client paperwork at the office, getting yourself or a loved one to a doctor's appointment in the middle of the day, or just getting your laundry done at home. We do these things, even when they're difficult to do, and even when the world *makes* them difficult to do, because they're important for the health and well-being of ourselves, our loved ones, and those we work with. Having good boundaries means distinguishing between what truly *needs* to be done and what's extra. *It means identifying what you're willing to compromise on and what you're not.* For the tasks on our list that simply must be done, it also involves asking ourselves how we might be able to bring more support, comfort, and ease into those experiences.

Making the distinction between what we really need to do and what we don't can be difficult for all of the reasons we've already discussed in this chapter. When I'm working with clients and supervisees on issues of bound-aries and responsibilities, I often use a version of Sage Grayson's exercise

"The Not-to-Do List."[33] This exercise helps people sort the tasks and issues they have in front of them into what they really do need to get done, what's beyond their control, and what could be done by someone else. It also helps people identify which tasks are especially difficult for them so they begin to understand where they might need to reach out for extra support. Working through this exercise helps turn an overwhelming to-do list into a concrete *not-to-do* list—a list of things that are not your responsibility, that don't need to be done right now (or that you don't need to do alone), and that are outside of your control (and about which you can, in fact, do nothing). This can help make the list of things you really *do* need to do less daunting.

Exercise: The Not-to-Do List

If you find yourself overloaded at work, try writing out on a sheet of paper, in point form, all the workplace tasks and issues that are weighing you down. This is your "to-do list," and the items on it could be expectations or responsibilities of any kind. Working

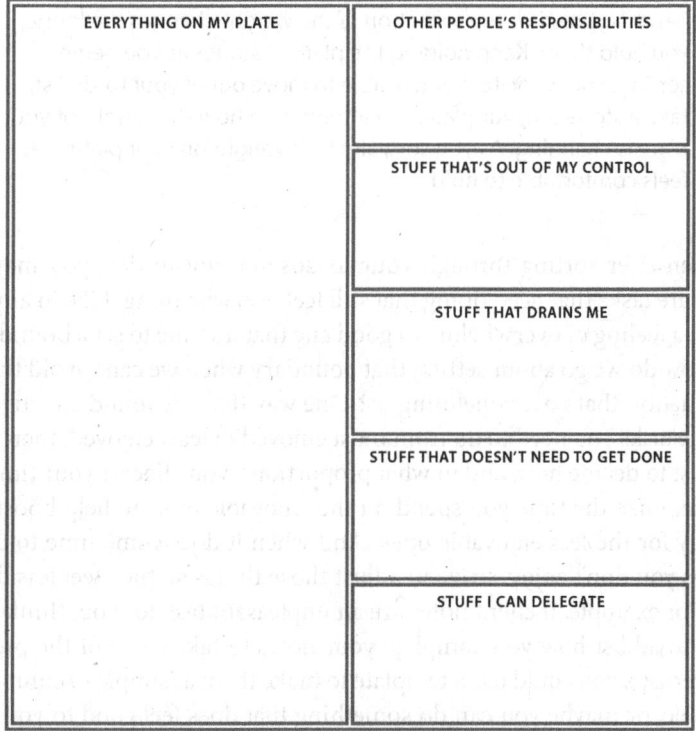

EVERYTHING ON MY PLATE	OTHER PEOPLE'S RESPONSIBILITIES
	STUFF THAT'S OUT OF MY CONTROL
	STUFF THAT DRAINS ME
	STUFF THAT DOESN'T NEED TO GET DONE
	STUFF I CAN DELEGATE

Adapted with permission from Sage Grayson, Life Editor (SageGrayson.com)

from the list you've created, sort each bullet point into one of
several categories: "other people's responsibilities," "stuff that's out
of my control," "stuff that drains me," "stuff that doesn't need to get
done," and "stuff I can delegate." When you move an item into one
of these categories, cross it off your to-do list. When you're done,
you'll be left with several lists—one of things you need to do, and
others of things that you don't (at least, not alone).

Exercise: Weighing Your Options

If you want to try an even more tangible version of a not-to-do
list exercise, consider this suggestion from my colleague Olga
Yakovlyeva: First, gather together about twenty to thirty small
stones or pebbles (you could also buy these at a dollar store) and
a paper plate. Hold the paper plate in one hand. For every item
on your to-do list, put one stone on the plate. Before you begin
sorting your tasks, carefully pick up your plate and really feel the
weight of the stones. Notice what it's like to hold them in your
hand. Notice how the sensation of the weight changes the longer
you hold them. Keep holding the plate of stones as you begin
sorting. For every item you're able to move out of your to-do list,
take a stone off your plate. Pay attention to how the weight of your
plate is changing. As you sort, aim for a weight on your plate that
feels comfortable to hold.

Even after sorting through your to-dos and not-to-dos, you may find
there are tasks that need doing that still feel overwhelming. Like in any situation, a feeling of overwhelm is a good cue that it's time to set a boundary—
but how do we go about setting that boundary when we can't avoid the task
or situation that's overwhelming us? One way that I've found effective is to
list the tasks you need to do from most enjoyed to least enjoyed, then to use
this list to decide how, and in what proportions, you allocate your time. Try
to maximize the time you spend on the enjoyable tasks to help boost your
energy for the less enjoyable ones. And when it does come time to do the
things you don't enjoy, strive to adjust those things so they feel less daunting. For example, if client notes are an unpleasant task for you, think about
ways to adjust how you complete your notes to take some of the pressure
off. Perhaps you could use a template to make them as simple to complete as
possible, or maybe you can do something that does feel good to you while
you complete your notes, such as setting yourself up in a cozy space or even
outside on a sunny day.

If you work with a team, or have the resources to create one, delegation can be another way to take some of the pressure of unpleasant tasks off your plate. Most psychologists I know who work in private practice eventually find that hiring a virtual assistant or office administrator is worth it, despite the cost, because it allows them to spend more of their time focused on the client work and on other aspects of their job that they enjoy. As you look at your list, you may want to consider whether hiring outside help could be beneficial to you.

Finally, when you're working to create boundaries that balance your responsibilities with your needs, it can be useful to reframe the responsibilities that you find difficult to fulfil and think about them in terms of their value. What will fulfilling this responsibility mean for you in the long term? How will it help you do or achieve things that you are able to give a whole-self yes to? What does fulfilling this responsibility do for you today? You might also try shifting the way you feel about certain tasks in the short term by emphasizing the ways in which the items on your to-do list are helpful to you rather than framing them only as things that need to get done.

A Pathway Forward

People often wonder how boundaries became such a struggle for them. They worry that the difficulty they have setting boundaries must mean that something's wrong with them, or that they're just not as strong as other people. Therapists, in particular, may wonder why they have such difficulties even though they understand the value of boundary-setting. I think the better question is: How could you *not* have difficulties? Even those of us with critical awareness of how our environment has shaped us are not immune to harmful cultural conditioning and structural issues. So many of us have been taught in so many ways to turn away from ourselves that I'm amazed when anyone comes into my office with relatively intact boundaries.

It can be both painful and difficult to get out of the pattern of putting ourselves last and take the risk of doing something different. Most of us will experience deep guilt and shame when we start respecting our boundaries. We're battling uphill against societal expectations that discourage boundary-setting and, as we've seen, there are real, structural barriers to contend with even at the top of that hill. When we try to introduce more sustainable practices, we risk significant psychological, social, and financial consequences. I invite you to reflect on whether your social conditioning and societal environments have led you into unnecessary suffering.

When people ask me, in various forms, "Is what I'm experiencing really bad enough to get help or say something?" what I really hear them saying is "Do you think I should just keep suffering?" Of course, my answer is no. We all need to decide what boundaries we feel safe enough to set on our path out of suffering, but it's important to be clear on one thing: You are allowed to have needs, no matter what society tells you. And you don't have to wait until things are at a breaking point to take a step back and take care of those needs.

One step that everyone can take is to slowly begin identifying and recognizing the messages we have picked up over the years about who we are and how we live our lives, both from other people and from the inequities we've experienced in society. While many of the social factors that underlie these messages are beyond our personal control, this is an exercise that *is* within our control, and that can help us let go of any shame we feel around our boundary struggles by situating the reasons for those struggles outside of ourselves. We can start to ask ourselves if the things we learned growing up are really in our best interest, or whether they serve someone else's need. We can question whether the things we choose to do in our lives reflect values that we hold, or values that someone or something else has held over us. From there, we can begin to get choosy about which messages we want to hang on to and which ones we're ready to let go of. And then, with time, we can work on believing something different.

An important element of this work, as Jordan Pickell writes, is giving yourself permission to evaluate your choices and your boundaries on your own terms:

> When you set boundaries, let go of trying to get [people] to admit you are right and they are wrong.
>
> When you set boundaries, let people have their feelings about it.
>
> When you set boundaries, let go of the belief that you have the power to control their behaviour.
>
> The essential assumption of boundary-setting is "I cannot control you, and you cannot control me."
>
> Your boundaries aren't right or wrong. They just are.[34]

Just as emotions aren't good or bad, boundaries aren't right or wrong. Let yourself release the shame of what should and shouldn't be. Instead, allow yourself to have needs without worrying whether they're right or wrong.

Boundary Practice

Choose two things you were taught growing up that you want to let go of. Write them down, in as much or little detail as you like.

Now it's time to get creative. Some people symbolize letting go by ripping up what they just wrote. Other people bury their writing. Personally, I'm a fan of a good old fashioned fire.

Whatever you do, let the ritual be something concrete. This is not just about saying to yourself that you're letting go. It's about actually doing something to represent the letting go—embodying the release.

When you're done, journal about your process. How do it feel to let go of these lessons? Get curious in a whole-body way: Ask your head, heart, and body.

5

Coping with Guilt and Shame

Many therapists struggle with boundaries because they experience guilt and shame when they set them, especially when they involve responsibilities to clients. We are especially vulnerable to guilt and shame of this kind when we aren't connected to ourselves and our core values—for instance, when we're using others' values and expectations, which don't necessarily align with our own, to guide us. To better understand how guilt and shame influence our boundaries, we need to get clear on what these emotions are and how they work. By shifting our relationship to guilt and shame, we can start to leave more room for ourselves and our boundaries.

Unpacking Guilt and Shame

True guilt is a healthy, adaptive response for humans that lets us know when we are doing something out of line with our values or otherwise making a mistake. I invite you to choose something in your work life that you are currently feeling "guilty" about and ask yourself, "Am I doing something out of line with my values?"

If the answer is yes, then you're dealing with what I term *healthy guilt*, and there's a lot we can do with that guilt. We can learn from it, repair the harm, make peace, reach out to others, and/or apologize to any aggrieved parties. We can also atone, forgive, pray, persevere, or accept ourselves as human. Now here's the part that gets tricky. Not all guilt is "healthy," and it can be difficult to distinguish healthy guilt from something more destructive. Most therapists I meet experience this difficulty, regardless of identity or background, but as clinical psychologist Harriet Lerner points out, there may be some gendered elements to destructive guilt as well: "Because women are encouraged to feel guilty about everything—and to take responsibility for all human problems—we often have difficulty sorting out when guilt is there for a good reason."[1] For Lerner, guilt is there for a "good reason" when it lets us know that the position or action we've taken in a particular situation or relationship is not "congruent with our own values and beliefs as we have struggled to formulate them, separate from pressures of family and culture."[2] These are the values and beliefs that we discover by reconnecting with ourselves through, for example, all of the practices already discussed in this book. Of course, it takes a lot of practice, patience, and courage to do the work of reconnection. Practice, patience, and courage are also needed to learn how to sort out your feelings of guilt—that is, to understand when you have a healthy relationship to guilt, and when that relationship is tied up in other people's expectations and beliefs that no longer serve you. I call this second type "the guilt trap."

We'll come back to the guilt trap shortly, but for now let's focus on healthy guilt. Take the example of having a hard time focusing in a session because there's something going on in your personal life that's taking your attention—a situation many therapists can relate to. Our loss of attention may not align with our value of being present with our clients, and this may bring up guilt. In this case, the guilt might say, "I want to be a therapist who is present with my clients in session." If you listen to that healthy guilt message, you can begin to think about how you can avoid similar situations in the future. For example, you might make sure to do some grounding and centring activities before you begin sessions, or you might decide to cancel a session if you know you won't be able to be present.

This isn't to say that guilt isn't a challenging feeling—it is, after all, not always easy to apologize and deal with our mistakes—but healthy guilt is relatively easy to work with. We can recognize it, and then choose what to do. When we allow ourselves to learn from it, it can get us back on course and support our well-being. This is corroborated by research. As Brené Brown has noted, healthy guilt that tells us when we are out of synch with our own values is inversely correlated with addiction, depression, violence, aggression, bullying, suicide, and eating disorders. As she puts it, "The ability to hold something we've done or failed to do up against who we want to be is…uncomfortable, but it's adaptive."[3] When we can accept our mistakes and our less-than-perfect behaviours with compassion and humility, we can let them bring us growth.

It's common to hear people equate guilt and shame, but I think of them as different experiences. There are many definitions of shame, and when people are describing their own experience of shame to me, I tend to follow their lead around what, exactly, it is. For clarity, though, I'll use a definition that is widely understood and accepted among therapists. Shame's distinguishing feature is intense and deep-seated beliefs about one's own worth: It is the intensely painful feeling or experience of believing that we are flawed and therefore unworthy of love and belonging. As Brené Brown puts it, while guilt is "I did something bad" or "I made a mistake," shame is "I am bad" and "I am a mistake."[4]

We don't just feel shame out of the blue, for no reason. Feeling shame comes from experiences of being shamed.[5] Although we are all born with the capacity to feel shame, we're not born *in* shame—that is, we don't come into this world feeling that we're somehow inadequate. We learn those messages over time from the people and situations around us. People shame others accidentally or purposefully all the time by equating who others *are* with what they've *done* (e.g., "How could you do that?" or "You're so self-ish"). Experiencing shame in this way can affect our sense of who we are as people and our ability to act. Instead of pressing pause to help us examine our behaviour (like healthy guilt), shame freezes us. It tells us to hide our-selves, to not let anyone see, to disappear, to clam up and keep it all inside. It tells us that we're bad, that something is wrong with us, and that we don't deserve kindness.[6] While healthy guilt has an adaptive function of mov-ing us away from something—ideally, away from unhelpful behaviours—shame moves us away from ourselves, and thus away from our own values and our understanding of our own limits. In this way, shame is a source of disconnection from ourselves first, and then from other people.

Experiences of shame are huge roadblocks in the process of learning to set boundaries. When speaking your own needs and setting a boundary to meet them brings up shame, you may feel compelled to move away from your needs and your boundaries. In other words, when you make a move toward being more "you," your shame puts up a barrier because it feels that the "you" you're moving toward is wrong.

When we're immersed in environments that are toxically shaming and the consequences of that shaming aren't repaired, the impact is significant. Deep shame, believing that at a core level there's something wrong with us, is also called identity trauma, and functions like other forms of trauma that we discussed in chapter 3. If this speaks to you, your first step in setting boundaries may be to work with a trauma-trained therapist on releasing the shame.

The Guilt Trap

Imagine that you have a client who requests a weekend session even though you've clearly communicated that you don't work on weekends. This client tells you it's the only time they can come this week, and they really need to see you. When you think about reiterating your boundary and saying no to the client, you feel a sharp twinge of guilt. So, you ask yourself: Am I doing something out of line with my values? Have I made a mistake? If the answers to these questions are "no," then where is this guilty feeling coming from?

Earlier, we defined guilt as a healthy feeling alerting you that you are acting out of line with your values. When you feel guilty in situations that don't seem to match that template, you may be caught in what I've come to call *the guilt trap* (figure 5.1).[7]

The way I define it, the guilt trap is not truly an emotion (though it absolutely feels awful). Instead, it's a pattern of thinking we can get caught in. There are two parts to this thinking trap: first, the thought that you're responsible for *fixing* other people's pain; and second, the thought that you're responsible for *causing* other people's pain.

If these thought patterns sound familiar, you are not alone. Many therapists who feel caught in guilt are in fact experiencing the guilt trap, especially when working with clients who are really struggling, and especially when expressing a boundary that they fear may cause a client disappointment or discomfort. For many people, and particularly for therapists, the guilt trap is not a one-off experience. It's a deeply ingrained habit of thinking. It can be tough to act differently than we're used to, even when we know we're not doing anything wrong. If you ever find yourself in this situation, the first step to getting out of the guilt trap is to simply recognize you're in it. From there, remind yourself that you are acting in line with your values to the best of your abilities, and remember two key truths:

1. Your role is not to fix other people's problems but to recognize and support their own innate capacity
2. You will disappoint people in your care, but you can do so with integrity.

The key words here are *capacity* and *integrity*. Let's look at each in more depth.

Capacity: Getting Out of the Fixing Role

If you identify with the thought that you're responsible for fixing other people, the way out of the trap is capacity—specifically, other people's capacity. I have had the incredible privilege of being let into hundreds of people's lives, and I can tell you this with certainty: People are incredibly resilient, creative, and smart. It may not always seem like it from the outside looking in—especially if we feel like we're responsible for fixing others' pain—but people are capable of way more than we tend to give them credit for.

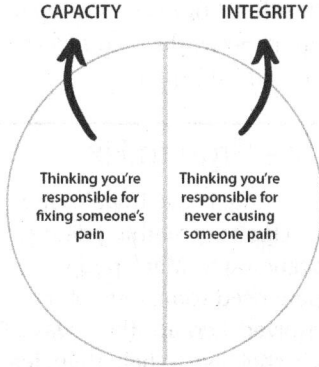

Figure 5.1 *The guilt trap*

When we walk into a relationship with the mentality that we need to fix something for the other person, we're essentially saying to them, "I don't believe you can do this yourself." We all get caught in this line of thinking every now and again, but recognize that it's unfair to both you and your client. When you take on the role of fixing things in another person's life, you don't leave room for them to take that role on for themselves, and nothing will change. And because you feel responsible for making something change, this will make you feel bad. I've worked with many people who keep hoping that, if they just give one more piece of advice or assistance, things will turn out okay. Persistence is not the answer; empowerment is. An empowerment-based framework suggests taking a step back and allowing the client to step into their own power.[8]

Remember, too, that people, regardless of age, generally don't like the idea that they're "broken" and in need of fixing, nor that they're incapable of helping themselves. If you've ever had a toddler in your life, you may be familiar with what happens when you try to do something for them that they can (or want to) do for themselves: They get downright angry at being made to feel powerless. I think this is also how a lot of adults feel when someone tries to do for them what they can do for themselves, though adults tend to be better at hiding it. The natural inclination for independence and a sense of self-efficacy shows up early on and persists throughout a person's lifetime. When you take on a fixing role as a therapist, it can frustrate this inclination in your clients.

Taking a step back from occupying a fixing role with a client can be challenging. Often, people feel threatened by changes in a relationship, even if the change is ultimately for the positive. You will need to be gentle with clients and prepare for potential push-back. Give your clients time to process the change and, as with other boundaries, prepare yourself to stick with it through practice, support networks, and lots of compassion. Take some deep breaths and remind yourself: *capacity*.

Trauma and the Urge to Fix

If we find ourselves saying "I have to help, and I'm the only one," this could be a clue to something deeper in our nervous system that needs tending to. Many people with these kinds of thoughts have experienced some form of trauma at an early age that hasn't been resolved. Perhaps there was a time when they needed the adults in their live to help them feel safe, but those adults weren't capable of being there, so they found another way to cope. A little voice inside of them said, "I need to fix this; I need to make the world a safer place." The second, silent part of that sentence is "because it's not safe now, and no one else is fixing it." This makes sense: children understand implicitly that if their parent is okay, they can be okay too, so if they *make* their parent okay, if they can "fix" their parent, they will secure their own safety as well.

In adulthood, the impulse to "fix" a parent can grow into an impulse to "fix" those around us. Whether those people are our parents or not, the impulse remains an expression of a need for safety, and the attempt to fix others is a strategy for feeling safe in the world. This strategy stems from a trauma mentality rooted in ongoing beliefs often rooted in a childhood experience: The world is inherently unsafe, I am the only person who can or will protect myself from it, and if I can make others safe I can make myself safe too.

When we approach our clients from a trauma mentality that pushes us to fix or save them, we cannot walk with them through their own trauma and suffering. If we're both stuck in the whirlpool of trauma, that means no one is standing on the edge, grounded and able to offer a connection to hope or aliveness. It's just two people caught in the waters. Though clients may not be able to name it directly, they will know the difference between being supported by someone who is empathizing with their pain and someone who is overtaken by it. Our clients pick up on our nervous system cues, whether we're in a calm place or a desperate one.

If you find yourself caught in a fixing mentality, it's possible to learn another strategy for feeling safe that will benefit both you and your client: self-regulation. We'll touch on this again in chapter 6.

Integrity: Understand That You Will Disappoint People in Your Care

If you're holding yourself up to a standard of never being allowed to disappoint others or cause them pain, understand that this is an impossible standard. No matter how conscientiously we approach counselling work, we will, at some point, disappoint clients or cause them pain. Disappointment is an unavoidable part of being in relationship with others. We have a limited amount of time and energy, we make mistakes, and we aren't the right therapist for every client. As social worker Nedra Tawwab writes, "You can be a 'good' person and still do things that others won't like. There is no way to spare someone's feelings when you say something that they don't like. Even when stated kindly, some things are hard to receive."[9]

Sometimes, people's disappointment is a reaction to our boundaries. To avoid causing this kind of disappointment, many people get caught up in seeking others' permission to set a boundary. The belief is "If I get permission, my boundary won't hurt or disappoint the person who has permitted it." Often, this belief is not in our best interest. Not only does getting permission not guarantee that the other person won't be disappointed, but the permission itself is not guaranteed; if we need the permission to set the boundary, we may never set it. Remind yourself that other people don't have to understand your boundaries. Your boundaries are the right boundaries because they are yours, even if others dislike them or disagree.

Fortunately, there's a way to handle causing pain and disappointment that reduces the negative impact for both parties. If you find yourself frozen by the possibility of disappointing others, you can help yourself out of the trap by acting with integrity: treating the other person with kindness and respect and acting in line with your values. Imagine waking up sick on a fully booked day of sessions and knowing that your schedule is full for the next few weeks. Acting with integrity might mean staying home and resting to protect your health and that of your clients, even though you don't have an immediate option for them to rebook. It might also involve managing your schedule differently in the future so that there's more leeway for life to arise.

Reflect and Journal

- Can you relate to the thought that you should be responsible for fixing others' pain? What about the thought that you are responsible for never causing other people to hurt? How has that trapped you in guilt?
- Think of a time in your work as a therapist where you can identify being caught in the guilt trap. How might focusing on your own integrity and the capacity of others have changed this situation for you?

Perhaps a conflict of interest arises with a new client. Acting with integrity might look like informing them early, giving good referrals to another therapist, and ending the relationship rather than waiting for a problem to arise. When we act with integrity, even when we're saying no or having difficult conversations or causing disappointment, we can feel proud of how we handle things.

Guilt over Resentment

Breaking any habit can feel uncomfortable, and getting out of destructive habits of thinking is no exception. At first, sticking with your boundaries may be an unpleasant experience, and you may feel guilty for doing it. Practice saying to yourself, "I am acting in line with my values to the best of my ability." Practice saying, "Other people have capacity, even if I cannot yet see it." Apply some self-compassion. Remember that this discomfort, though unpleasant, is not an indication that you're a bad therapist. You can practice setting boundaries *and* be a good therapist.

Practice truly is key here. It's one thing to know on an intellectual level that having boundaries and being a good therapist are compatible truths; it's another to really feel, experientially, that the sentiment is true. The more you practice setting and honouring your boundaries, the less discomfort you're likely to feel. You will see from your experience that you can remain compassionate, connected, and generous while still being able to have human limits. Eventually, saying no to the things that overstep your boundaries becomes a way to honour your body's wisdom. It becomes a way to make room for something better.

If you're still not sold on the idea that you can move past the discomfort of disappointing a client, remember that if you're ignoring your own needs, you're already feeling uncomfortable. Setting boundaries and potentially disappointing others is just a different kind of discomfort: one that will ultimately heal and pass with time. And as uncomfortable as it is, especially at first, it may just be the best option you have. As Gabor Maté writes, the alternative is resentment:

> A therapist once said to me, "If you face the choice between feeling guilt and resentment, choose the guilt every time." It is wisdom I have passed on to many others since. If a refusal saddles you with guilt, while consent leaves resentment in its wake, opt for the guilt.
>
> Resentment is soul suicide.[10]

This idea has always resonated with me on a gut level. Both healthy guilt and the guilt trap are things we can work through with practice, reminders of our humanity, and actions that are in line with our values, but resentment will eat at you and at your relationships. It deeply impacts our sense of and trust in others, leaving us feeling disconnected. Without connection to others, resentment can be very difficult to recover from.

Brené Brown reminds us that, although boundary-setting can be a struggle, it ultimately creates the pathway to kinder and more loving connections: "We let people do things that are not okay, or get away with behaviors that are not okay, then we're just resentful and hateful. Me, I'd rather be loving and generous and very straightforward with what's okay and what's not okay... So now I think I am not as sweet as I used to be, but I am far more loving."[11] Here, Brown draws a distinction between being nice and being kind. For her, being nice is about pleasing others, often to your own detriment, in order to look good. It's saying "I don't mind" when, clearly, you do. If we extend ourselves beyond our capacity like this, we will end up under-resourced and less available to those we are trying to help. We may end up feeling resentful toward the clients we are trying to be nice to, even when we are the ones deciding what we offer. Being kind is different: It's about extending human empathy and compassion, yet holding boundaries that respect what we're willing and able to do—another way of saying acting with integrity.

When we work from a place of wanting to be nice, we prioritize what's best for our client or employer and use this to guide how we work. Some therapists allow their booking to be wide open even if they don't want to work evening hours, or allow a client to continue booking future appointments when they haven't paid for previous ones, because not doing so makes them feel selfish. Some may accept contracts where they don't agree with the terms out of a feeling of obligation. We don't necessarily think about what these ways of working might cost us or the resentment they may seed. Even though it might be uncomfortable at first, remember that it's kinder to yourself and to others to respect your own boundaries by making a change in a relationship where resentment is beginning to blossom rather than allowing that resentment to continue growing.

Reflect and Journal

- Think about the phrase "Boundaries are about doing the kind thing." What does this mean to you?
- What would it look like for you in this season of your career to choose guilt over resentment?

Moving Through Guilt in Life-or-Death Situations

It is particularly common for therapists to feel caught in the guilt trap when working with clients who are really suffering. It's important to underline for therapists that the process of boundary-setting is not just for low-stakes situations, but for all situations, including those that involve serious risk such as client suicidality and intimate partner violence. In this line of work, you will likely find yourself with not just one situation like this but many, for years on end. We can't help but think about our clients in between sessions and, especially for our vulnerable clients, worry about their safety.

Moving through guilt can be particularly difficult in life-or-death situations. Sometimes people feel that if they know what's happening with a client between sessions, they'll feel better. It's true that client updates—like when we get an email from a vulnerable client who we haven't heard from in a long time—can be temporarily calming. But constant monitoring can also leave people feeling worn out. Maybe you're already emotionally drained from supporting a client through an initial crisis, in part because you put some other aspects of your work and life on hold while they worked through it. Saying yes to a one-time crisis situation in this way may be within many of our boundaries, but saying yes every day, as much as we might want to, is bound to become impossible. More than likely, you will come to a point where you really wish you had more to give but need to say no. Figuring out how to say no when you need to is the only way to keep doing the work, even when the stakes are high.

Counsellors need to abandon the idea that we can control our clients or their decisions—even decisions as big as whether or not they decide to keep living. Yes, we must abide by our professional code of ethics and intervene if the client is in immediate danger of hurting themselves or someone else, but at some point, we all need to get clear on what we can offer to our clients beyond this, regardless of the situations they are in. At baseline, our offers often include bearing witness, providing space for reflection, offering pathways to healing, and giving advice when requested. No matter how much we might wish for it to be different, we can't keep another person alive. In fact, attempts to do so risk creating a situation of resentment and distance between a therapist and client. By stepping over the boundaries of a therapeutic relationship and trying to control someone else's life, we end up making ourselves and the other person unhappy, and a truly supportive, therapeutic, and trusting relationship slides further and further away from us.

When the stakes feel high, it's normal for boundary-setting to be a particular struggle. Yet these are exactly the kinds of situations in which we need boundaries the most. They call on our humanity and our empathy, and we can't bring those things into relationship without boundaries. Brené Brown discovered this in her research: "One of the most shocking findings of my work was the idea that the most compassionate people I have interviewed over the last thirteen years were also the absolutely most boundaried."[12] This statement might seem counterintuitive if we've learned to believe that compassion and empathy are only possible when we open ourselves, unbounded, to others, but hopefully, at this point in the book, you're starting to see some truth in it.

Self-Forgiveness to Unlock Shame and Rewrite the Narrative

As you begin the process of setting boundaries in your personal and professional lives, you may also need to begin learning a process of self-forgiveness. Specifically, you may need to learn to forgive yourself for not being able to be everything for someone, for not being superhuman, and for not having unlimited time and energy. You may also need to learn to forgive yourself for the boundaries you have not, until now, set. It is so easy to let shame take over when you realize how drained and resentful you've been. There might be a part of you saying, "I should have done this sooner" or "I've wasted all that time." We can recognize that this voice, though it may be trying to protect us, is instead keeping us stuck in shame. Continuing to heal and move forward means forgiving yourself for not knowing some of this sooner and for sacrificing so much for so long.

Part of self-forgiveness may also involve rewriting the narrative you're telling yourself. So often, we label ourselves, or are labelled by others, as somehow "less than" when we say no and don't live up to our standards of the perfect helper. It's possible to redefine it in a more positive light. For instance, would it work to practice seeing yourself as a therapist who's getting clear about their needs? A therapist who is doing their best, even when they make mistakes? A therapist who is deeply human? Here are some shame-free narratives that I've adopted in my practice:

- We are all only human.
- We are doing the best we can (with the time, energy, and resources we have available).
- We will make mistakes.

I know at times it doesn't feel like we're allowed to be anything but perfect. As we discussed in chapter 4, there are reasons for this: we live in a world that tells us (in a thousand different ways) *not* to have compassion for our mistakes or to care for ourselves—not in a way that's actually nourishing, anyway. In fact, sometimes we are outright shamed by others (e.g., "Wow, you're leaving early" or "I wish I could do that but I have a lot more work to do"). Cultural norms have made it uncomfortable for many of us to be human, have needs, and take up space. This is why shame and guilt-trap thinking are major obstacles to setting good boundaries. But as Sonya Renee Taylor reminds us, the idea of taking up too much space or having too many needs really doesn't hold water, especially when you consider how much space and how many resources some folks are already taking: "Take a moment to consider that space is actually infinite, right? The notion of 'taking too much space' is born out of a framework of scarcity upon which we have built a world where some people are allowed to build skyscrapers and stadiums or run countries and make laws for the masses, while others are told to stay small, go unnoticed, don't take up too much room on the sidewalk."[13] I read this quote as a call for us all—clients, therapists, and other humans alike—to let ourselves take up more space. I often say to my clients that taking up more space does not mean pretending you are *more important* than other people (a thought that can be pretty unpalatable for empathetic people!); it means that you are *just as important* as other people. It's ultimately about treating yourself as an equal.

Many therapists of my acquaintance—including myself—agree with the idea that we are all human and are allowed to make mistakes, yet they simultaneously hold different standards for themselves. Many of us are so tuned into the pain of those around us that we can start to separate the categories of "humans who struggle" and "humans who help," placing ourselves in the latter. This self-othering has consequences for our well-being. For one, it justifies the habit of denying ourselves the kind of care and allowance for struggle that we afford to others, which can easily lead to burnout, resentment, and despair. More insidiously, when we start to other ourselves, we place emotional distance between ourselves and the people around us who are struggling. That distance is the first step in losing empathy for our fellow humans. If we want to stay in connection and continue doing the good work we do as therapists, we need to treat ourselves as we would treat our clients: with care, compassion, and respect.

Boundary Practice

Using any of the ideas in this chapter as starting points, create your own, unique, shame-free beliefs to support you in setting boundaries. Post them somewhere you need the reminder and share them with the support people you chose in chapter 1. Keep in mind that part of believing something new is having new experiences. Make decisions that are in line with your new beliefs.

PART II

Practical Boundaries for Practising Therapists

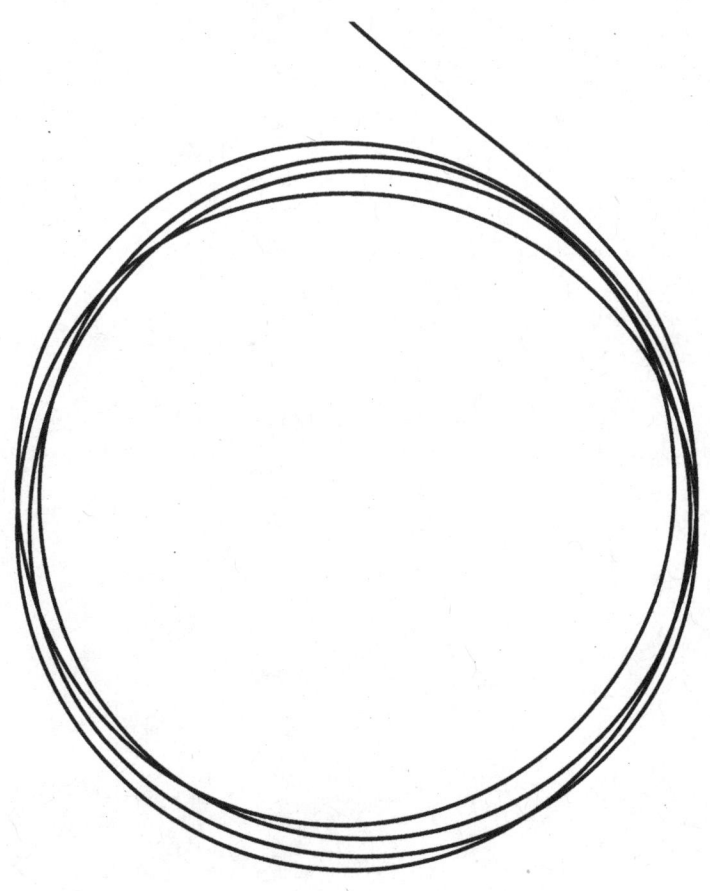

6

Boundaries Around Our Emotions

Being affected by our clients is a good thing. We're human, and a lot of what we witness with clients is bound to move us. We experience joy, connection, and moments of laughter along with them. The experiences we have in the therapy room impact us, from how we feel immediately after a session to how we see the world and what we understand about what it means to be human.

I want you to continually be moved and transformed by your clients. I want your clients to feel really seen and loved and understood. After all, as therapists, connecting with others on these deep, meaningful levels is literally part of our job. But there's a fine line we all have to walk between connecting with others and losing track of ourselves, and it's important to remember that, if we do lose track of ourselves, we also lose the quality of our connection with others. To make deep connection an ongoing reality in your practice, it's crucial to learn how to stay open to and empathize with others without going under. I want to offer a vision of empathy that helps us stay connected with ourselves while *also* connecting with clients.

One of the best ways each of us can foster these two kinds of connection over the long term is to develop and maintain emotional boundaries that are a good personal fit. Developing these boundaries can feel uncomfortable, especially for therapists who, through experience and training, have learned to equate emotional boundaries with coldness, detachment, and barriers to connection. Remember: Boundaries are not antithetical to the connection and empathy work we do; they are integral to that work. They allow us to connect by protecting us from injury and by connecting us with ourselves. Emotional boundaries, in particular, help us protect our emotional energy by allowing us to connect with others without feeling overwhelmed by their pain. They help us to be present alongside someone without being consumed by their experience.

This chapter offers some ideas about how to bridge the gap between therapist and client without losing touch with ourselves. The first step is understanding how and why we can lose ourselves in attempts to connect with clients.

Merging, Joining, and Disengaging: How We Stand in Relation to Others

Somatic experiencing has taught me that there's a difference between, on the one hand, joining with a person we're caring for in a way that feels safe and connected for both of us and, on the other, merging with them.[1] By merging, I mean inadvertently taking on or mirroring processes in the other person's nervous system. When we merge, we move from empathizing with another person's feelings, listening to them, and providing a calm, regulated space in which they can share their experience (i.e., joining) to *actually feeling* the other person's feelings as if they are our own. We may start to experience body sensations, too, as though we are not just hearing about a situation in another person's life but are actually experiencing the situation ourselves. For example, you may be merging with a client if, when that client begins to feel anxious and finds themselves short of breath, you notice chest tightness and shallow breathing in yourself. If the person you're speaking with is lost in despair with slumped shoulders and a closed-off posture, you might notice your own body collapsing. When our minds and bodies begin to mirror and mimic our clients' experiences, we begin to lose our boundaries and ourselves.

One way to understand merging is as a somatic way of "walking a mile in someone else's shoes." This is an approach to empathy that researchers have called imagine-self perspective taking (ISPT), and as a strategy for connecting with others, is likely very familiar to most people in Western culture.[2] It's no surprise, then, that many working therapists have found themselves in the merged position at one point or another. It's particularly common for therapists who struggle with boundaries. But as evidence shows, imagining what it would be like to experience someone else's trauma both puts us at risk for vicarious trauma and isn't very effective.[3] Therapists who use this approach often get it wrong when it comes to what their client is feeling. Studies have shown that ISPT decreases our overall accuracy when trying to perceive another person's feelings and preferences while also occasionally increasing confidence in our judgment. Meanwhile, asking for another person's perspective through conversation increases accuracy.

Often, the experience of merging goes hand-in-hand with the experience of disengagement—the opposite of the connection that merging sets out to create. Disengagement is conceptually similar to burnout, as described in chapter 1. Signs of disengagement included feelings of helplessness and a desire to give up. You might frequently catch your mind wandering while your client is talking, or find yourself wishing we were somewhere else. Being in the merged position can become so draining that, consciously or unconsciously, we may feel our only option for protecting ourselves is to cut ourselves off from the emotions and experiences of other people so that we don't have to feel them. This can create a flip-flop dynamic: Merging is overwhelming so we disconnect. But disconnection doesn't feel good either, so we eventually begin to seek out connection by merging, and the process begins again. Ironically, neither of these strategies serve us well. Merging does not create the connection we're seeking, and disconnection does not heal our overwhelm. Healing depends on human connection and presence.

Developing personal, emotional boundaries help us spend less and less time being merged or disengaged and more and more time being joined: reaching out to the other person *from where we are* and *as who we are*, rather than seeking connection by, in effect, *being* the other person. Joining is an act of bridging, from one person to another. It requires that we ground ourselves in our own nervous systems, in our own bodies, in the here and now, and that we are able to differentiate between the other person's experience and our own. An image I use to think of joining is sitting in my own seat rather than sharing a seat with my client. From my own seat, I can have my own perspective. I can connect with my own breath and comfortably feel my feet on the floor. I can notice the

Reflect and Journal

Imagine yourself standing on the edge of a riverbank. From the bank, you can see a person caught in a whirlpool and struggling. You jump in and get swept up in the current with them. Check in with yourself. What's happening in your body as you imagine this?

Now imagine that instead of jumping into the whirlpool, you reach out to the person from the safety of the bank, your arms outstretched but your feet firmly anchored. Check in with yourself again—how does this scenario make you feel?

The first scenario represents the merged position; the second represents the joined position. How did your experience of these two positions differ?

things I can see from my seat, which help to remind me of where I am and of the unique window I have onto the world, including onto my client's experience. When we join with our clients, we don't have their experience; we witness it. Maintaining our own perspectives in this way makes it easier to stay hopeful and curious.

The joined position fits well with an approach to empathy that researchers have called imagine-other perspective taking (IOPT).[4] IOPT contrasts with ISPT. Whereas in ISPT we immerse ourselves in another's experience, in IOPT we get curios about what the experience was like for the other person: observing, inferring, and asking questions about how the other person feels. It is difficult to stay open to and curious about someone's experience when you're immersed in it, but staying open and curious is, like connection, an essential part of the work of a therapist. If we lose our perspective and curiosity, we begin to find ourselves struggling against the current of another person's trauma rather than standing on the shore, where we can reach in and support them. IOPT helps us stay in the joined position.

Noticing When We Are Merging

Being able to notice when you are merging with a client is an important step towards protecting your emotional energy. At first, this practice needs to be an extremely conscious one. I encourage therapists, both during and after sessions, to make explicit efforts to notice what's happening in their embodied selves—that is, their head, heart, and body—and what's happening with their attention.

Noticing the Embodied Self

During each session, regularly check in with your inner experience: Track your emotions, behaviours, and physical sensations, and practice naming what you are experiencing. Purposefully check in with yourself and watch for any change in activation, such as a faster heartbeat, quickening speech, or a tightness in your chest. Check for feelings of urgency and for impulses to fix a situation, or the other person, or yourself. Notice if you're feeling hopeless, stuck, or unclear. Any of these signs are clues that you may be in the merged position.

Also allow yourself to also watch for emotions and experiences like ease, comfort, and openness. Notice if you feel connected to both yourself and the client, and pay attention to feelings of slowing down and attuning to what the client needs. Any of these may be signs of being in the joined position.

Each person is different in terms of how their nervous system reacts to particular situations and how those reactions manifest in their thoughts, feelings, and bodies. We are also all different in terms of how we can bring ourselves back to a joined position when we notice we are losing ourselves into a merged position. For me, when I am more activated, I notice my body leaning toward the client. I find that physically leaning back and grounding myself in my chair helps me return to the joined position. It may take some time for you to recognize your body signs and how best to respond to them, but I encourage you to consciously and intentionally practice. Having language for our experiences and attending to what's happening inside ourselves is the first step to being able to give ourselves what we need. Once you are clear on how you currently stand in relation to your clients and how this position manifests in a embodied way, you have more room to set and maintain emotional boundaries that keep you sustainably connected and engaged.

Attending to Our Attention

We've already talked about attention in terms of disengagement: finding our minds wandering away from our clients is a way of protecting ourselves from the overwhelm of merging with their experience. Noticing where we are focusing our attention is also an important part of noticing when we are in a merged position. When we're working with clients who've experienced trauma, for example, it's easy for our attention to go toward and get stuck on the devastation of the experience.[5] Getting out of the merged position does not involve entirely redirecting our attention away from the trauma experience—that would be disengaging—but it does involve attending to what else is present in the client's experience. Perhaps the client is feeling hopeless—that needs to be acknowledged. But it's also important to notice and be curious about how they managed to survive.

It is common for therapists, especially new ones, to struggle with attention in session, not because they get lost in a particular aspect of the client's experience, but because they get caught up in thoughts about how they're doing as a therapist, or what they should be doing in a session. If this happens to you, remember that, more than having the perfect words or deploying the perfect techniques, it's how we show up with our clients and make ourselves available for connection that makes the biggest difference in their care. Personally, I'm available to show up for my clients as Nicole, a person who sometimes makes mistakes and gets it wrong. That's different than showing up as The Psychologist with All the Answers—a pressure most people cannot sustain for long. As therapists, it is not our job to fix clients' circumstances or take on their pain for them. Our job is to offer a safe place where clients can experience co-regulation: a process of being soothed by the presence of another, more regulated nervous system.

Attending to our attention is also important outside of sessions. Helping professionals may need to be conscientious about what they expose themselves to and what they spend their attention on outside of session. As I've written elsewhere, "If we surround ourselves with trauma in our work, home, news media, and so on, we can start to lose hope. Many helping professionals active in the field of trauma choose not to read the news. Or, they may take breaks from reading about certain subjects or watching TV or movies that are violent. Protecting ourselves from exposure to too much traumatic content is one way to protect our hope and help ensure we do not become traumatized ourselves."[6]

Protecting yourself from trauma by carefully attending to your own attention is important to the care you provide to your clients. Curiosity, hopefulness, and our own aliveness are antidotes to the trauma, and will allow us to stay in the joined position more often.[7] They are what allow us to bring a bright infusion of humanity even into the dark our clients may be walking through. The time you spend exposing your client to a healthy nervous system can be a crucial factor in their healing.

> ### Reflect and Journal
> - Where does your attention tend to go when you are with clients?
> - What are some of your whole-body signs that you're merging with a client?

Returning to the Joined Position

The joined position is where we're aiming to be most of the time with clients. It's the position from which we can be clear on both our own needs and what's happening for clients because it's a position from which we can maintain our own perspective without being caught up in the experience of our clients. Ultimately, the joined position is a place in which we recognize, trust, and respect our own emotional boundaries.

A few strategies for returning to the joined position from a position of merging or disengaging have already come up throughout this chapter. To those, I'd like to offer a few specific and practical strategies that can be deployed any time you notice yourself losing connection with your boundaried self.

Give Yourself Time

Often when scheduling clients, early-career clinicians simply adopt the schedule they've been given by administrators. While administrators can do so much to support clinical work, they don't necessarily have an in-depth understanding of the time we need to do the various aspects of our jobs, including taking care of our physical and emotional well-being. We need to be the ones to advocate for the time we need.

If you can, leave yourself time before each session to engage in grounding and regulating practices such as breathing, movement, or mindfulness. If this time isn't already provided to you, consider speaking with your employer about the importance of spacing your sessions so that you don't feel rushed. Ask yourself how much time you realistically need before you begin seeing clients for the day and between each client. Personally, I like having thirty minutes before the first session begins to set up, orient to the space, and settle in without feeling rushed. Experiment with what works best for you, leading with the idea of spaciousness. Experiment, too, with giving yourself time within therapy sessions to come back to yourself and the session. Take a moment for yourself: Sit back in your chair, feel your feet on the floor, and slow down what you were saying.

Finally, ensure you schedule time for yourself at the end of your workday to comfortably finish what you need to do (such as finishing up notes) and to decompress (such as by acknowledging any feelings that came up for you during sessions and are lingering). Allowing yourself time to decompress can fit well with a practice of containment: an activity or ritual, such as lighting a candle, writing in a journal, putting objects away, using imagination, or doing physical movement, that helps you keep any work-related emotions at work so they don't follow you into the rest of your life. (We'll talk more about containment in chapter 7.) Noticing and naming what you're feeling can help you emotionally put the work away. It's important that you make space for this wind-down in one form or another. Remind yourself that you have done enough for the day and can come back to the feelings you've named the next time you're at work.

Reflect and Journal

- What helps you decompress between clients so you can be present and connected with the person in front of you?
- What helps you to decompress at the end of the day so that you can be present in the rest of your life?
- Do you have a containing practice of your own? What is it? If you don't, or if you'd like to try a new practice, what could such a practice look like for you?

Practice Grounding and Orienting

To feel more grounded and to regulate your nervous system during tough sessions, use your five senses. Common techniques we can use both with clients and with ourselves include the 5-4-3-2-1 technique, rubbing or pressing palms together, tapping your feet on the ground, or letting your eyes move toward the most comfortable part of the room. Grounding exercises will help you reorient to your own perspective and allow you to notice what you can see that the client cannot. They help you to truly be in your own seat—to feel your feet on the ground and your back supported by the chair, to tune into your own sensory experience. Grounding yourself helps your body remember that you are in your own present moment, not inside the client's experience of the past or present.

Exercise: A Grounding Technique

In this exercise, take the time to notice (out loud) what you're aware of through your senses. Go through each sense one by one. You can name anything that you notice, or you can focus on the things that are most comforting. Between each of your senses, take a breath and a moment to remind yourself where you are. I invite you to try this exercise now and see what your experience of it is. Do you feel any more relaxed, grounded, or present?

When you practice grounding yourself in session, you can name what you're doing out loud, if you'd like. Doing so can give the client the opportunity to ground themselves, as well. You can also practice grounding techniques silently, while still listening to what the client is saying. When you can feel your feet rooted into the floor and your breath slow and calm in your chest, you're on the right track.

For many people, grounding practices don't come easily, especially if they have been disconnected from their bodies (see chapter 3). They may be something you choose to work on in your own personal therapy so that they're more practiced when you go to sit down with clients.

Reflect and Journal

How do you ground yourself in the here and now, when you notice that you're taking on the emotional state of the client?

Reflect on Your Role

How would you name your role as a helping professional? Are you an expert, a guide, a helper, a collaborator? All of these? Something else entirely?

The way we view ourselves in our work reflects our particular mindset toward the work, and it very likely influences our ability to continue with it. Remember what we talked about in the last chapter: Whatever your role is, it does not involve fixing. Rather, it involves helping people to recognize, connect with, and apply their own capacity.

Having the impulse to fix others, or understanding one's role as being a fixer, is not unique to therapists. Neurodivergent writer and teacher Meg Berryman describes how the impulse to fix caused her to burn out, even after she changed the type of work that she was doing and shifted from a job within a larger organization to working for herself. Though what she was working on had changed, the *way* she was doing her work hadn't: "It was still an adrenaline-fuelled, urgency-riddled affair involving lots of busy work...I had no boss, but I had internalised the expression of one and used it to punish, belittle and shame myself for not working enough, not knowing everything and not growing my business as fast as others could."[8] As Berryman makes clear, our external environment can have a big impact on how we view our role, and especially on the messages about roles and responsibilities that we internalize in the first place. We must examine what, exactly, we've internalized and whether we agree with those messages before we can start changing them for ourselves.

In a study on burnout and growth among Australian psychologists, several participants described how establishing and maintaining boundaries and shifting their perception of their role—in particular, letting go of personal responsibility for clients' safety and well-being outside the therapy room—was essential to being able to sustainably continue their work.[9] Many participants in the study also discussed how they felt the sustainability of their work improved when they were able to shift their understanding of their role away from large, aspirational achievements rooted in fixing (such as "change the world" or "save everyone") and toward something smaller.[10] This sentiment was reflected in another study about vicarious resilience in psychologists who do trauma work, which highlighted more relational roles, like sharing journeys and serving others. One participant noted that "a sustaining aspect of trauma work was her belief in the therapeutic relationship as the primary 'vehicle of change.'"[11]

Imagining ourselves as fixers or saviours is a sure-fire path to burnout and away from deep relation and connection. Thinking of our roles in ways that allow us to set and maintain emotional boundaries will protect us from injury and allow us to truly be in relation with our clients over the span of an entire career. When I, for example, am connected to my wise, grounded self, I know in my whole body that it's okay to say no. I can hold onto myself in the face of other peoples' disappointment. I can say no and still be a good person and a good therapist. I can know that I'm doing enough and that doesn't mean I have to be doing it all. And you can, too.

You'll notice as you read through the rest of the chapters in this section that the different types of boundaries and needs we may have around our work—the boundaries around our emotions, time and attention, workplace, and finances—all overlap and interact with one another. The time we give to work will impact how much we earn, and thus overlaps with our financial needs and boundaries. As we discussed in this chapter, it will also impact how much time we are able to give to taking care of our emotional and physical selves. Our attention needs and boundaries intersect with what our workplace is like, what it demands of us, and how we interact with it. Changes in our available time and finances may influence our capacity to be fully present in our work, whether it's more or less. While we are looking, in part II of this book, at specific areas where boundaries will be important in a therapist's career, it's important to notice the interconnections of these boundaries, and to note again that a boundary, regardless of its target, is an embodied decision that affects us in wholistic ways.

Boundary Practice

Using inspiration from the exercises described above, choose one activity to help you remain in or return to your window of tolerance. It can be something new, or something you already do and that you would like to do more consistently. Practice it daily for a week and see how your nervous system responds. What impact does a regulating practice have on your ability to set boundaries?

7

Boundaries Around Our Time and Attention

Most of us become therapists because we believe in the power of the work and the importance of offering a container for healing. We spend years of our lives training for the job and many more years being in relationship with people who we support. We're here because we've decided that supporting psychological health is worth what we give to it. If we didn't care, we wouldn't be here to begin with.

It's no wonder, then, that it's so difficult to put limits around our time and attention. Many of us have never explicitly learned how to be in relationship with others while also having limits. But just like our clients, we're human, and we only have so much we can give. Even when we technically have the time for another hour of work, it doesn't mean we are capable in any real way of giving it. The time demands and the emotional strain of pushing past our limits have concrete effects on our home life and individual health.[1]

As we discussed in chapter 1, setting boundaries isn't just about saying no; it's also about making room for yes. In a culture that thrives on busyness, it's especially important to think about how you will protect your time from being taken over by work. It's important to feel that you have time to slow down and tune in to both yourself and the person sitting across from you, and it's important to spend as much time as you can on activities you enjoy, both at and outside work. When we're mindful of our time boundaries, these things are possible.

Time boundaries relate to the amount of time spent engaging in work. This includes direct client work as well as indirect client work such as case notes, consultation, and training. It also accounts for time we spend thinking or worrying about work—in other words, our attention. As highlighted in chapter 3, the cultural prioritization of productivity over health can lead us to ignore our boundaries. We spend more time doing than being, and this is particularly challenging in workplaces that already have a problem with task or project overload, including many non-profit agencies and public health organizations. What's more, there are systems at play in our society that are vying for our attention all the time. In his book *Stolen Focus*, journalist Johann Hari discusses his findings from more that 250 studies on attention and concludes that people are struggling with focus and attention more and more, as illustrated by increasing reports of being unable to read for a sustained period of time and having a constantly wandering mind. The many interviews that Hari has conducted on the subject bear out this finding. The reason for our collective struggle with focus, he suggests, is multifaceted, and includes a general increase in levels of physical and mental exhaustion and the rise of digital technologies that are designed to track your habits and manipulate your attention.[2] As these factors wear down our ability to focus on what we want or need to focus on, we may need more time to actually get our work done, and end up giving that work more time than we are willing or reasonably able to give it. This, of course, feeds right

Reflect and Journal

Have you ever:
- ☐ Felt like you weren't doing enough?
- ☐ Had a hard time sitting down and relaxing, even when other people were doing so?
- ☐ Felt exhausted but unable to stop because the work wasn't done?
- ☐ Felt guilty saying no to extra projects at work, even if saying yes would mean you'd have to volunteer your time without pay, or work overtime?
- ☐ Found yourself unable to relax because of everything on the to-do list you "should" be doing?
- ☐ Gone to work even when you were sick?
- ☐ Ignored a basic need like hunger or thirst because you were "too busy working"?
- ☐ Denied yourself rest or disallowed breaks, even when your focus was starting to falter?

For the items you said yes to, answer the following questions to guide your reflection.
- Describe what you were experiencing inside, emotionally and physically. What effect did it have on you to prioritize productivity over health?
- Are there certain situations or environments in which you find you are more likely to overstep your boundaries around time and attention?

back into the mental and physical exhaustion that is contributing to our lack of focus.

Difficulties managing our time and attention are common experiences for those living in a culture of constant busyness. These difficulties can be further exacerbated by feelings of obligation and guilt around what we're able to get done within a certain timeframe. Therapists are certainly not immune to these experiences. Luckily, we can learn to better understand and manage our time and attention so that they work for *us* rather than for some other person or system beyond us.

Assess How Your Time Is Split

Within the broader scope of our lives, we need to consider where our time and attention is going. In helping professions, it isn't uncommon to spend excessive time and attention on work-related tasks and concerns, both on and off the job. Ask yourself:

- How often am I checking work email outside of work hours?
- How many nights a week do I engage in work-related tasks at home rather than spend that time on myself or the people I love?
- How much time do I spend thinking or worrying about work when I'm not actually at work?

Some therapists I've spoken with find an imbalance in the time and attention they give to work compared to other things in their lives. This imbalance can leave them so overwhelmed that, paradoxically, it even begins to limit their ability to actually get their work done. Remember: Engaging mentally in work while not physically *at* work—by thinking about tomorrow's to-do list, for example, or worrying about the well-being of one of your clients—is still work. Purely mental work can be just as draining as actually being at work, if not more. This is true even at a neurochemical level: Just thinking about a stressful event will produce the same level of cortisol as physically being in that stressful environment.[3]

Other therapists are able to maintain focus, even hyperfocus, at work, but the degree to which it drains them leaves them disconnected from other important areas of their lives once they're off the clock. They can get work done in one area of their life but not in others, and they struggle to find the time to really relax. This means that even therapists who experience a flow state at work need to think about how long they can sustain that state without it interfering with their life outside of work.

If you've been feeling short on time, scattered, overworked, unbalanced, or exhausted, practice noticing how much time you spend both physically and mentally at work. Think about how much attention you give to work on your off-hours and keep track of the time you spend on specific work tasks during the week—for example, time spent with clients, on administration, on professional development, on practicum requirements, on teaching or research, and on advocacy. Which activities or tasks are most draining, and how much time are you giving to them?

It is also important to remember that our workload includes responsibilities outside of work. Many therapists I know are juggling parenting, caregiving for aging parents, health challenges, and other family and personal responsibilities with their professional responsibilities. These workload factors outside of the workplace are often what necessitate boundaries at work. For example, one study on Canadian psychologist mothers reported that many participants wanted the option of working part-time. Others shared dissatisfaction with childcare hours and noted that they had difficulty completing their work within these hours. On-site childcare was seen to be beneficial, and the absence of it, at least for one participant, was the reason she left her job.[4] The study highlighted that an employer's willingness to flexibly accommodate the needs of these psychologists was essential to retaining them as employees.

Assess Your Needs

Setting time boundaries also requires that we understand what our time needs are. For example, you might ask yourself how you need to divide your time before, during, and after sessions to be able to focus your attention on your clients. Do you need to check emails before sessions begin to get them off the table or do you prefer to do them all at the end of each day, after sessions are over? Do you need to close your eyes and mentally regroup between sessions or do you need to use this time to do paperwork so you aren't worried about completing it at the end of the day? Do you need to set aside time between sessions or in your daily schedule to have regular snacks and full lunches so you aren't distracted by hunger? Do you need to start or end work earlier? Do you need to work partial days?

You may also ask yourself how many clients you can feasibly see per day and still retain energy afterward to engage in the activities you enjoy and to take care of important life tasks. How many per week? It is normal, especially for those who work primarily with trauma or complex cases, for this number to be relatively low—a fact that will have an impact on your finances. Some therapists choose to deal with this by having a job that allows them to balance their schedules with different types of clients. Some choose to have more than one workplace, each with different tasks and responsibilities, to add variety to their work week. Some supplement their work with different types of offerings, like groups or workshops.

Whatever you choose, be mindful. The point of assessing your time and attention needs in your current work situation is not to fill all the gaps in your schedule with more or different work just because you can. Sometimes we do need to fill some gaps to address other needs, such as those around finances and income, but if you're considering taking on an extra project, whether it's because you have the time or need the income, consider carefully how this new work will fit into your life:

- How does this project fit into your existing workload? What time and energy do you have available for it?
- Does this extra project align with the values you have for your work? Does it connect with how you want to spend your time?

What Are You Willing and Able to Give?

In your role as a therapist, it's important to continually to check in with your capacity, in terms of both what you're willing and what you're able to give. Willingness is about what we're prepared to offer wholeheartedly and without resentment. Being willing also means not attaching expectations of gratitude, results, or reciprocity to what we are offering. We do something willingly if we do it because *we* want to do it for its or our own sake.

Ability is about what we're capable of doing without harming ourselves. When we think about what we're able to do, we need to account for our limited time, energy, and resources. If doing something comes at great cost to you (emotionally, physically, or otherwise), then you may not really be able to give it, even if, technically, you "can" and you "have the time." Many people have about sixteen waking hours every day, but I don't know anyone in this profession who can engage in productive, mindful work for that amount of time. Sixteen hours of focused work is beyond most people's ability.

Reflect and Journal

What are you willing and able to give in your role as a therapist? Where do your willingness and ability overlap and where do they diverge? Use the following chart, adapted from change-readiness assessments used in organizational psychology, to map out what you are and are not currently willing and able to give at work.

Able and willing	Able but not willing
Not able but willing	Not able and not willing

In my work and relationships with supervisees and other counsellors, I have noticed how burnout affects our willingness and ability. As we give more and more time and attention to work, beyond what we are able and perhaps even willing to give in the first place, we become less and less willing to give any more. It's normal for those already burnt out to have difficulty coming up with many things they are truly willing to give. By contrast, those with strong boundaries around the time and attention they are willing and able to give to their work also, perhaps surprisingly, have an abundance of willingness for the work they are doing. Because they're not extending themselves beyond their ability, they have more life energy and more capacity, both in and out of the workplace.

Time and Attention Boundaries for Students and Provisional Therapists

Being a student in counselling or psychology is a one of the most challenging periods in the profession in terms of boundaries around our time and attention. Coursework alone can be a lot to handle, and you may be juggling it with thesis writing and practicum hours on top of your non-school responsibilities. This is partly because of a culture within academia that encourages working at all hours, every day of the week, and generally having few or no boundaries around time or energy when it comes to your studies (something that would, in a non-academic context, be quickly labelled a toxic work environment).[5] Many also struggle with the extremely competitive nature of many academic environments. To compete with peers for spots in certain graduate programs, practicum placements, and jobs, many of my supervisees report that, as students, they took on extra training (at their own cost) and volunteer work on top of their studies to set themselves apart.

Being a provisional therapist is another very challenging time. The first five years after graduation can be a steep learning curve accompanied by external pressures to gain experience in a wide range of issues and to work as much as you can. You may be trying to balance seeing clients with time spent studying for licensing exams, receiving supervision, and taking training. It can be easy to get swept up in the unspoken expectations of employers and colleagues to work long or unusual hours, or to take on every client who walks through the door in order to fill an agency need, collect hours, or generally make a good impression at your workplace.

Sometimes, the push to do more and say yes at these career stages comes from a fear of missing out on opportunities that you feel could get you ahead.

But it's important to consider whether you're able to give an embodied-self yes to the opportunities that come up. If you aren't, those opportunities may not, in fact, be right for you right now. That's okay. Continue following your path, guided by your boundaries. There is always more work to do; there are always more opportunities to be had.

Keep in mind that practicing from a state of burnout makes it difficult to take in learning and experiences of growth. It seems counterintuitive, then, that the learning environments we often find ourselves in are so unbounded. School, training, and provisional hours can feel like a full-out sprint, but a common refrain in my group of colleagues is that this profession is a marathon, not a sprint. As one colleague, Susan Larcombe, specified, this means that it needs to be built sustainably from the start, as much as possible.

A key word there is *possible*, though as another colleague of mine astutely pointed out to me, recognizing possibilities can be a challenge: "When I work with master's students (as clients) or provisional psychologists (as their supervisor), they kind of roll their eyes at the encouragement toward self-care, as it seems so impossible in the face of completing all of their graduate school work or supervised hours while also making a sufficient income to survive. This is a conundrum." It is exceptionally difficult to manage boundaries in many school and early-career environments. Remember, though, that this difficulty is a reflection of the environments, not of you. Also remember that there really are things you *can* do to make a bit more room for yourself. Prioritize finding a place of work that will pay you enough without requiring you to work beyond your capacity. Seek out peers, advisors, colleagues, mentors, professors, and supervisors who see you as a human first, a student or provisional therapist second. Familiarize yourself with any accessibility or other accommodations available at your school, practicum, or workplace that could give you more control over your time and attention. Focus on your needs and take seriously your willingness and ability to do the work in front of you or to take on one more thing. Working and learning within your boundaries is not a matter of giving up on the hard work of your education or falling behind in a competitive environment; it is what will allow you to flourish in your academic and professional growth.

Reflect and Journal

- If you're in school, how do you protect your time and energy?
- What boundaries do you already have in place that work for you?
- How do you make decisions about which learning opportunities to take on, and which to say no to?
- What are your time and financial budgets for new learning and training?

First-Person Perspectives

Initially I found it somewhat challenging to set boundaries around work times. In my program, we have client hour quotas for every semester when we are on practicum. Particularly when I first started seeing clients, I would offer them just about any time when the clinic was open and I was not in class for sessions. I wanted to make sure I was being flexible and accommodating of their schedules, and I figured that by keeping my availability open, I would have more bookings and less concern about meeting the quota. This got challenging at times, since travelling to the clinic to see a single client was not an efficient use of time that could have otherwise been spent doing coursework or taking a break. After getting more comfortable with client work and clinic logistics, I began limiting my availability to both ensure I had a range of days and time slots open for clients, but also making sure I was leaving myself time for other things.

I found it helpful to define the days where I would see clients and the days where I would not. I learned to recognize that my clients would be okay if there was a week or two where their schedules changed and they were unable to book sessions within my available time slots. By setting this boundary, I found I was better able to take care of myself and complete other responsibilities. I think that having my set days off and knowing I would have that time helped me recharge and ultimately made me more prepared and engaged for my sessions. It's easy to burnout or experience trauma fatigue in this profession, and having days to myself made a big difference for me.

—*Mark, Clinical Psychology Student*

Setting Time Boundaries at Work

The idea of setting boundaries related to work can feel daunting, and sometimes people aren't sure where to start.

The following are some basic suggestions to help you start thinking about time boundaries at work. Start small and start with what is immediately under your control. The time-related factors that you control on the job may differ from workplace to workplace—for example, not every job allows for an hour-long lunchbreak, lets employees choose the number of clients they see per day, or allows employees to work flexible hours—so some of these suggestions may not be open to you right now. Adapt them to your situation and your own personal needs, but keep the spirit of this suggestion in mind: Take real, intentional time during your day, every day, to address your basic needs and care for yourself.

1. Let yourself have a bathroom break on a regular basis (as in, at least every few hours). Set yourself up for success by setting a timer on your phone and committing to follow through with it, even if you're in the "flow of work," even if you "could hold it a bit longer," and even if it's "not wildly convenient" (e.g., in the middle of a client session).

2. Give yourself a ten-minute, dedicated stretch or relaxation break after each session. Research suggests that focusing on one specific task and then taking time to mentally rest helps increase our productivity and sustain our energy. In one study, therapists who treat trauma in private practice discussed prescheduling extra time between a trauma session and their next client, even if the next client is not working on trauma, in order to have time and space to care for themselves in ways that will allow them to be present for other clients.[6]

3. Have a specific time each day that you take your lunch, and take the full time. Do so away from your desk and away from all technology. Go outside if possible. This is your time to be with yourself. Enjoy your food and allow your brain the time it needs to background-process what's already happened rather than continuing to actively work.

4. Leave work on time every day, even if the work is not "done."

Containing Your Work

Containment—the ability to delimit certain thoughts, feelings, or memories so we can choose when to experience them fully—is in an important tool that I teach to clients. I often work with clients who have experienced trauma and have not yet found a way to contain it. They might feel unable to stop thinking about a traumatic event, which causes them to constantly relive or re-experience past pain or to be overwhelmed by emotion. Without containment, trauma can take over a person's life.

Containment is also an important tool for therapists. On top of being humans with limits and needs around our time and attention, we work with people who are struggling, and this is immensely emotional work. Due to our exposure to traumatic events through our work, we are at higher risk of vicarious trauma. Containment allows us to honour what we're experiencing inside—our stresses, our concerns, our to-do lists, our anxieties—while also allowing us the latitude to choose when and where we work on or pay attention to certain things.

One technique I use with clients is having them imagine a physical container in which they can store their difficult memories. It can be any shape, size, or colour; it just needs to be big enough to hold the memories, and there needs to be a way to close or secure it. Depending on what the person is struggling with, they can sometimes find it difficult to imagine a box that's big enough for all of their memoires. If that's the case, I ask them to imagine a box that's bigger on the inside than on the outside. (To all the *Doctor Who* fans out there, yes, your box could definitely be a TARDIS!) Though the container can be closed, it's not meant to be locked away forever. Instead, it's meant to be a safe place where a person can keep memories between sessions and something that they can access and open when they choose to. Creating a container can help people gain a bit more control over just how and when they work with difficult memories.

Therapists can use this technique for difficult memories and for other purposes. For instance, I use the same technique when talking to my supervisees about boundaries around work and attention. Containment can help counsellors pack up their work *mentally* when they pack it up *physically*. It can help clearly define when and where work is and is not, and what thoughts, emotions, memories, and experiences belong in the workspace but not out of it. Like it can do for trauma clients and their traumatic memories, containment can help therapists prevent their work from taking over their lives.

Containment practices may also include structures and practices in our work life that help underscore, for ourselves and others, the difference between work time and personal time. To give you some ideas of where you might begin, here are some practical strategies I use to contain my own work:

- Avoid checking emails or answering phone calls outside of office hours. If it helps, keep your work emails off your phone.
- Invest in a work-specific phoneline so you can keep business and personal separate.
- Communicate your office hours clearly with clients and give them information about who to contact outside of those hours in an emergency. Remember that you *are* allowed to have these limits. (A sign in my child's medical clinic reminded all patients that the physicians "take

Reflect and Journal

- Have you set any time or attention boundaries in your work environment before? How did they help you work in a way that's sustainable?
- What is one thing you could do, starting today, to better protect your time and attention?

no calls after hours." I thought, "If pediatricians can turn off their phones after hours, then the rest of us probably can too.")[7]

- Allot a specific amount of time each day or week to worry about work-related problems. Once that time is up, mindfully and consciously redirect your attention to the present moment.

When You Have a Home Office

For those who work fully or partially from a home office, the boundaries between work and home might feel even more blurry. It can be especially tough to "turn off" at the end of the workday and settle into home-mode or rest-mode. You may even feel guilty closing up your work.

To protect your boundaries in a home-office situation, make sure you create a workspace that is separate from your life space. It's hard to relax with a good book and catch up with a friend if you're in the exact same office chair or armchair you were in all day, completing your administrative work or seeing clients. If you have the space, whether you see clients from home or not, designate a room specifically as an office space, and nothing else. Set it up the way you like it. If you don't have space for a separate office but would still like an area where you can do administrative work from home, you can get creative. You could designate a specific part of one room in your home for work and use it exclusively for that. If you're working with an especially tight space, you could sit on one side of a table while you're in work mode and another side while in home-mode. Or maybe you have one laptop that is only for work and another one that is for personal time. Whatever your situation, the idea remains the same: establishing specific spaces or orientations in your home that are exclusively for work tasks and nothing else can help you contain your work to work time, even when work time happens in the home.

Transitioning from Work to Home

The way you move through the liminal space between work and home is key to how you approach your work-related time and attention boundaries. To support this transition, I suggest setting up routines that let you move between different spaces not only physically, but also emotionally and mentally.

My transition-to-work routine is pretty straightforward when I'm working from home. It starts with putting away distractions: giving myself time to wrap up conversations or let people know I'm unavailable, and turning my devices to "do not disturb." When I'm dealing with home or personal stressors, giving ample time to acknowledge and contain them before work is a must, as it makes it less likely that they will seep into my conscious attention while I'm trying to focus on a client. Then it's time to transition into work mode, which I do by getting dressed in work clothes, turning on my scent diffuser, plugging in all my devices, getting some water, and locking the door to my office so I can't be disturbed. If I'm transitioning to a space outside of the house, I have learned to give myself ample time on both ends. For me, this means not booking clients right at the beginning of my day or right at the end. I arrange my schedule to have thirty minutes before my first client so that my nervous system has time to settle, and thirty minutes after my last client so I don't feel rushed finishing up and closing the office.

Transitioning from work to home at the end of the day has a bit more to it. Whether I'm in my home office or out of the house, I close down the programs that I've been using, respond to any emails I need to respond to before the end of the day, write down any to-do items I want to remember for another day, then turn off my computer and clear my desk. Some days, I will sit at my chair and write some feelings from the day, taking time to be with any difficult emotions I may have witnessed. Sometimes, I walk with the feelings, letting them flow through me physically instead of writing them down. Once I've given myself time to be done with work, it's time to prepare myself for being at home. That means making a commitment to not check my work email or work phone. The after-hours email from that co-worker or client can wait until tomorrow. If thoughts about work arise, I choose to let them keep floating by without getting caught up in them. Then I leave the office, whether that office is in my house or somewhere else, and commit to not going back to it until it's time for work again.

The overarching idea is simple: When you're at work, let yourself be at work. When you're at home, let yourself be at home. But simple or not, it takes practice, and some days and situations are easier than others. As with everything, go slow. The goal here is not to completely overturn your existing strategies for getting into and out of work mode, but to develop sustainable strategies and routines that will reliably support those transitions in the long term.

If, while reading this chapter, you caught yourself thinking, "I can't do these things at my work," take a moment to interrogate that thought and make sure that it really reflects your situation. It may really be true that you can't. There are real barriers in our lives and work that need to be taken into account, and that might mean that your ideal time and attention boundaries aren't feasible in your current work situation. At the same time, it is sometimes the case that we've never thought to ask ourselves or the people in charge if our current situation could be different. Consider asking. Sometimes the answer will surprise you.

You may find some of the suggestions and examples offered in this chapter harder to implement than others, or you may find that none of them work for you. That's okay. Identify something that you think could work. It should feel like a challenge, but a small one; it should still feel doable. Give that one small thing a go. You can always add more from there, when you're ready.

Boundary Practice

First, congratulate yourself for taking the time to read and reflect on your needs as a therapist. Hurrah! Now, let's keep going with the amazing work you've started. Choose one time-related boundary to practice this week. Record your observations.

8

Boundaries Around Our Workplaces and Finances

It can be easy to feel that, because our clients need something, we need to be the one to give it to them. I hear new therapists say things like, "They need evening hours; they can't make it during the normal workday" or "They need a sliding scale; they can't afford the full fee." And it's true: A client may really need these things. Some clients are dealing with financial insecurity and would be at risk of losing their jobs if they had to take appointment hours during the workday. Some clients have such tight budgets that they'd have to give up some of the essentials to make it to even an hour of therapy per month. Others need to cancel regularly at the last minute because they're dealing with chronic pain or illness.

There are absolutely times where we can meet a client on these things, for instance by giving a sliding scale where we can for the clients who need it most. But we also need to remember that we are not the one and only person who can solve these problems or fill these gaps for our community. Consistently overriding our own needs to meet the needs of others is not sustainable for us, and is thus not a sustainable way to address these issues for our clients.

We need to be asking questions about what conditions we, as the practitioners, need in a workplace in order to thrive. We also need to address what will sustain us financially. For our work to be sustainable, for us to be able to keep showing up to *do* this work, the day-to-day of our work environment and our compensation must be acceptable to us.

Many supervisees I've worked with focus on their employer's needs in the workplace over their own. But acceptable and sustainable work also involves having an employer that acknowledges and meets *our* needs. Just because an employer needs (or wants) something from us doesn't mean we will be willing or able to offer it—see the discussion of willingness and ability in chapter 7. For example, an employer may need coverage on weekends, but this may not match your need for you-time or for family time. Or an employer might want someone who can see a certain number of clients per day, or work with certain populations (e.g., children, families, individuals, or relationships), but these may not fit within your capacity and scope, and they may not be what you signed up for in the first place.

In this chapter, we'll explore some ways to examine and establish financial and workplace needs both as an employee in a larger organization and as a private practitioner, and we'll touch on some challenges and possibilities of workplace boundaries for students and those in supervised practice. The goal, like elsewhere in this book, is to try not to get caught up in what other people expect you to offer or accept, but to begin from a grounded understanding of your own needs and, from there, negotiate a relationship with finances and work.

Assess Your Workplace Values and Needs

To begin to understand what type of workplace may best suit you if you don't already have an idea of this—and really, even if you do—start with your values. As research has shown, getting clear on one's own values reduces stress, inspires better health habits, and boosts decision-making, problem-solving, and willpower.[1] Getting clear on our workplace value allows us to make wiser career and work choices.

What do I mean when I say "workplace values"? Here are some examples:

- Independence and autonomy
- Connection with others
- Flexibility

- Accessibility
- Comfort
- Slowness and ease
- Challenge
- Support

- Reliability/ structure
- Responsibility to clients
- Life balance

These likely don't all resonate with you, and you probably have others to add to this list that will better define what you, personally, value in a workplace. Values are meant to reflect what's important to *you*, not to your family, your colleagues, your employer, or your clients. Exploring your values is not about what you think *should* be important or what you *wish* was more important to you. Ask yourself instead, "If I didn't have to worry about what others might think or how they would cope, what would I want?"

If possible, zero in on three central, guiding values you have around work. (There may be a lot that's important to you, but not everything can be the most important.) Now think about what you might need from a workplace to support each value. If you value flexibility, an ideal workplace might be one that allows you to work from home and shift your schedule as needed (though be mindful of your time boundaries: having too much flexibility in the hours we can expect to work in a given week can make it hard to establish a routine). If you value comfort, you may look for a workplace with large windows, lamps, cozy seating, and good air conditioning or heating. If you value autonomy, you might lean toward monthly rental of a space so that you can retain control over how many clients you see, the work you do with them, your rate, and so on. These are, of course, not the only options; there are many ways a workplace might support any given value.

If you are still figuring out what you value in a workplace, look back at previous work, internship, or even school experiences to get a sense of what has and hasn't served you in past workplaces. Start by reflecting on a work situation that was not so good, and what about it was most challenging. Then, think of the best workplace you ever had, and what made it so enjoyable.

Reflect and Journal

- Reflect on each of your three top workplace value. What do they mean to you? Why are they important? Why did you choose them?
- Choose one of your values, and reflect on the following:

  - If you are currently working, how are you already organizing work around this value? List three things you could do at your job to better align your work with this value.
  - If you are a student or are looking for work, name three concrete things you could look for in a workplace to support this value.

Compromise and Non-negotiables

While we can advocate for our workplaces to become more accessible and accommodating of workers' needs and limits, organizational change isn't immediate or easy. Because burnout can be so closely tied to workplace factors, and many of these factors are outside of our immediate control, avoiding workplace burnout can be particularly challenging. This is where boundaries play an essential role. Boundaries can help us get clear about what we are and are not able to abide at our jobs and what we are and are not able to control in our situation while we continue to push for more accommodating workplaces. I like to think of boundaries in this context as creating a plan for sustainably existing in the world as it is while still working on greater change.

In any workplace environment, it is essential to ask yourself where you would be willing to compromise and what your non-negotiables are. A non-negotiable is exactly what it sounds like. If I decide that working on weekends is a non-negotiable because that's time I spend with friends and family, it means that I will not accept a job that requires weekends, even if it's the only job in my field that I can find at that time.

Not everything, however, will be non-negotiable. Even if we have an idea of what our ideal job or workplace looks like, most of us are willing to be flexible in certain areas. These are areas where we can practice compromise. I might prefer not to work evenings, but perhaps I'm willing to do so if a job comes up that otherwise meets my needs.

It's rare for a job to immediately be a perfect fit, at least at first, so it's important to understand your negotiables and non-negotiables so that you can take on opportunities that may work for you and avoid work situations that will truly be a bad fit. This is one area that can be challenging, especially for new therapists. When we feel financial pressure or are taught to believe that we should be grateful for any offer of employment, we can end up accepting work with which we are not okay. Many early-career therapists do so from a place of anxiety, desperation, and fear that nothing else will come along. Many therapists, new or not, do so out of real financial need. Of course, taking a job that oversteps our boundaries because we feel we have no choice means that our yes isn't a decision made with our whole, embodied selves, but one based on fear and scarcity. When we say this kind of yes, it may temporarily relieve our anxiety or material need, but that relief can quickly shift into resentment and burnout. These situations arise out of circumstances in which our needs and values conflict and there is no perfect solution. As in embodied decision-making, the key is to avoid ignoring one part of ourselves in favor of another. Ask yourself: Is there a way to honour all of the conflicting parts of myself in some way, even if not perfectly?

Employment decisions need to come from a mindful and grounded place where our eyes are open, we fully understand what we are signing up for, and we accept any compromises we may have to make and what we will receive in return. Even in very difficult situations, it's important to notice that there *are* choices to be made, and what those choices are. It's important to feel we have truly chosen for ourselves at work even when the choices are not perfect.

Your Workplace Needs in Action

Once you're clear on what you value in a workplace, it's important to think about what type of environment you would like to work in. Common environments for therapists include working for an agency or government organization, working in a group practice for a percentage, renting in a group practice for a set fee, or owning and operating a private practice of one's own.

Whatever you choose, do your research and, to the best of your ability, give yourself options. If you are planning to work for an employer, apply to multiple workplaces and go on several job interviews. Give yourself the best chance you can to have more than one job offer to choose from. If you're building a private practice, view at least three spaces to get a good idea of what's available in the market. Be ready, in all cases, to ask questions that will help you get to know a workplace better, and to better assess whether it meets your needs. (Some of these questions will apply to practicum experiences, too). These questions are important when you're moving to a new job or space, but can also be a great way to reassess the fit of your current job or workplace. Consider asking yourself these questions at least yearly, especially in the lead-up to or immediate aftermath of major changes in other areas of your life (e.g., changes in your health, family structure, living situation, and so on). What was a good fit at one point may not be a good fit forever.

In an employment situation, consider asking the employer and/or yourself:

- What are the policies around sick days and time off? (E.g., Do I need a doctor's note in order to take a sick day? Is there any limit to the amount of sick time I'm allowed?)
- What populations will I be working with?
- What kinds of client issues are most prominent?
- How much supervisory support is available?
- What kinds of opportunities are there for peer connection and consultation?
- Are there any training opportunities available?
- What are the expected hours of work, caseload, and schedule of clients in a given day? What does a typical week look like?
- What degree of flexibility does the job allow (e.g., hours, opportunity for work from home)?
- How much control will I have over the type of work I do and the clientele I see? (E.g., Am I expected to work from a particular model, regardless of fit for clients? If I am assigned or meet with a client who is outside my expertise or comfort level or is simply not the best fit, what procedures am I expected to follow?)
- What other supports are available to support my learning and growth?

- Are any benefits offered at this workplace, such as vacation pay or extended health benefits?
- Are there any formal policies in place around worker health and well-being? (And do these policies align with a practice that would be sustainable for me?)

In a private practice scenario, ask yourself:

- How far is the commute to the office?
- In a group practice, what are the opportunities for peer connection, training, or support?
- Does the space meet my comfort and/or accessibility needs? (E.g., Are there elevators or ramps? Is the lighting appropriate? Is the temperature okay?)

Workplace Tips for Practicum Students and Supervised Practice

I encourage students to apply to several practicum sites or organizations so they can really get an understanding of what's out there. Talk to peers and experienced practitioners in the field to help you understand common fee arrangements and expectations. In addition to the general questions to ask in an employment situation, listed above, you might want to ask about the number of direct client hours expected of you. Does the workplace leave time for doing coursework, receiving supervision, or studying for licensing exams?

Early-career practica and supervision can be extremely challenging and overloaded times. As one of my colleagues has pointed out, her supervisees are often working seven days a week, straddling two practices, and trying to complete their licensing exam. These comments underline the importance of asking questions and discovering what options are available to you in terms of practicum placements and supervision. You need to be able to make decisions that are, as much as possible, appropriate to you and your own needs and limits. As my colleague highlighted to me, "Every practitioner's nervous system is different and some can handle high-intensity demands more readily than others. As a supervisor, I ask practitioners to check in with their own nervous systems to attune to what feels best for them. Practitioners need to be self-regulated and grounded to be able to offer co-regulation to clients."

If you are already working or in a practicum, there's still time to reflect:

- To what extent do you feel supported by your employer and colleagues in setting boundaries and maintaining a sustainable practice? Do they model this, or have other explicit practices in place?

- What challenges have you encountered in trying to maintain a sustainable practice?

If you are entering supervised practice, give some special attention to the process of choosing a supervisor. Though some workplaces may offer supervision on-site, free of charge, you may want to consider whether this is the best fit for you. External supervision, offered by a therapist who does not work at your organization, is also an option, and can offer some important benefits. An external supervisor gives you the opportunity to connect with someone who may work in a very different way than your other colleagues, which means they can bring in a unique perspective. As someone who likely doesn't know your colleagues, they can also offer a relatively unbiased perspective. External supervision avoids the potential conflict of roles that can arise in on-site supervision (for example, being supervised by someone who is also your direct employer), which may allow you to speak a little more freely about your practicum experience and any difficulties you might be having in the work environment. On-site supervision has its own benefits. For example, it can be quite cost-saving if it is included as part of your contract. It may also allow you to access supervision more immediately and informally, whenever you need it.

When searching for a supervisor, internally or externally, ask yourself what's important for you in a supervisory relationship. For example, some people may want a lot of hands-on support while others are looking for more freedom to try things out. Some people might want support in a particular modality while others are more focused on ensuring the supervisor, regardless of orientation, is someone they can trust and feel supported by. To help you find a good supervisory match, consider asking potential supervisors some of the following questions:

- What is your philosophy on supervision?
- What is your style of supervision (live observation, case consultation, group, experiential practice in a particular model, co-therapy, observation of the supervisor, etc.)?
- What populations do you work with and what clinical expertise do you have? (And ask yourself: What populations am I interested in learning about? What clinical expertise would I like to gain?)
- What is the cost of supervision?

Keep in mind that your licensing body likely has a minimum supervisory requirement for provisional therapists. In Alberta, where I am based, the College of Alberta Psychologists stipulates a minimum of one hour of supervision for every fifteen hours of practice. Keep in mind that this is a *minimum.* While the minimum is sufficient for new therapists who prefer more unguided freedom to grow into themselves, many people benefit from more supervision than this, especially at first. For this reason, many of the supervisors I know suggest frontloading extra supervision as you're getting started, then tapering off to the minimum as you gain experience and confidence.

First-Person Perspectives

I recall early in my career when I was being supervised as a provisional psychologist, my supervisor informed me that I had the right to set boundaries with my clients including with whom I wanted to work. She noted that if I don't feel comfortable with a client, I am not going to do good work. This has stayed with me through my career, and I try to listen to my "gut feeling" when setting up an initial appointment with a client.

I talk a lot about "initial conditions" with my clients and supervisees, i.e., what you establish initially is what others will come to expect from you (not that you can't change your mind, but that it can be more difficult). Setting your boundaries clearly from the start can manage expectations. I have learned that it's better to be up front and clear from the start.

—*Andrea, Registered Psychologist*

The main issue within my workplace is that, while I have had a solo practice for a number of years, my office is in a wellness centre with other types of practitioners who have a different code of ethics with different boundaries—for example, midwives, who don't practice the same type of confidentiality, have the same understanding of time boundaries, or have the same professional boundaries around dual relationships. This has led to some difficult but necessary conversations about information sharing, avoiding dual relationships, and time boundaries.

—*Claire Wilde, MEd, RPsych, CST*

Revising Our Relationship with Money

Financial needs are an enormous consideration when it comes to workplace boundaries. Most of us are so familiar with the standardized eight-hour day, forty-hour work week, with two weeks' vacation a year that we do not always pause to consider whether that fits with the life we desire and can sustain.

Though there are financial realities to contend with, I still recommend taking the time to reflect on what is most important to you in life: What are your yeses, and how might work fit into that vision? Everything in your work should be built around your needs as a human—emotional, physical, financial, and spiritual—and the fact that these needs are interconnected.

What's Enough?

In any work situation, you must get clear on what's "enough" for you financially. What is the baseline for actually meeting your financial needs? I suggest creating a budget based on your past year and having a realistic look at your home and work expenses. If you're in private practice, your work expenses may include rent, office supplies, training, membership dues, taxes, and insurance. Looking at your income over the course of the entire year is also helpful because many therapists see large fluctuations from month to month (e.g., because client work may be slower in summer months, or because of a vacation).

A key piece of guidance: It's important to base your budget on a realistic month, not an ideal month. A realistic budget accounts for fluctuations in income based on both predictable and unforeseen circumstances. It should account for regular vacation days, sick days, and client cancellations, especially if these affect your wage or salary, or if you're in private practice. Remember that if a budget only works if you and your family members don't get sick, you do not have a workable budget.

For most people, it's also important to make room in their for savings for donations, joy and pleasure, or just to have a buffer. This amount will differ for each person, depending on their values, future plans, and risk tolerance, among other factors. It can be easy to feel that more is always better, especially if you have experienced tight financial times, but I encourage you not to let this perspective push you into work that oversteps your boundaries or forces you to set aside your non-negotiables. We need to think not only of what more money will give to us, but also what it will take away (e.g., time for health, connection, or joy). Think carefully about how much really *is* enough for you.

When it comes to financial needs, remember: Money does not equal worth. At the same time, compromising our financial stability is not a useful path toward justice. Finding ways to balance these two realities is important to developing sustainable financial boundaries.

Money Does Not Equal Worth

One piece of advice I commonly hear is "Charge what you're worth." Whether you're a private practitioner or and employee, the sentiment behind it is the same: Recognize your time and expertise as valuable and insist on a fee schedule or salary that reflects that value. We must consider the years of schooling we receive, the ongoing training we do throughout our careers, and the specialized mix of art and science that makes us unique as practitioners.

It is important to understand the value of our work and training. Still, I think the advice to "charge what you're worth" misses the mark. The worthiness equation ends up implying that our value, as people and professionals, can be equated to a particular dollar amount. It also risks implying that someone who gets paid less by the hour is worth less. If we are to maintain our sense of humanity, we cannot associate human worthiness, ours or others', with dollar amounts.

It's also important to remember that our sense of personal worth may ebb and flow. Our sense of ourselves is so often based on how effective we've been in the previous hour or our client's most recent assessment of their progress, and we're bound to have difficult client days. But while our sense of self may shift on a daily basis, it is likely that our budget is not so fickle. Making pricing or salary decisions based on our own or someone else's subjective opinion of us is more than complicated; it has real, material consequences on our livelihood.

Making decisions based on subjective ideas of worth does not, for instance, take into account the realities of living with chronic pain or health issues. It does not take into account the challenges and different financial needs of those who are the sole income earners for their families, or who may be supporting members of their extended families. It does not even, at a very basic level, take into account the cost of living. In short, tying one's income to one's sense of self doesn't account for any external societal factors that we don't individually control, nor our unique life circumstances. And it certainly doesn't account for personal financial needs, let alone our emotional, physical, or time boundaries. If we charge too little, it's very likely that our work will take up more time and energy than we're really able to give it—and that isn't sustainable.

What's more, relying on subjective evaluations of our monetary worth doesn't engage with or address our baseline relationship to money. Even if you're someone who assesses their value very highly and is comfortable charging "what you're worth," there's no guarantee that your assessment will translate into sustainable working habits. We live in a hustle culture— one that, as we explored in chapter 4, is more concerned with productivity and doing than with sustainability. Here, I appreciate the advice of Jen Carrington, a business coach who advocates for simplicity and spaciousness. Unlike other approaches to finances, Carrington's approach isn't centred on hustling to make the most money possible. She's a parent and human who lives with chronic illness, so her approach tends to align with the idea of sustainability. Though Carrington is coming from a business-focused rather than counselling-specific perspective, I think her perspective is valuable. Private practitioners *are*, after all, business owners, but the message also applies to work more broadly and is relevant to those who work for employers, too. As she suggests, it's important to build a work life that orbits one's broader life and oneself, not the other way around:

> Chronic illness or not, there are so many of us who just don't thrive at a go-go-go pace, who need spaciousness and rest built into our working lives for us to truly thrive along the way.
>
> …
>
> The only way I've made it here is by ripping up the able-bodied rulebook of what it has to look like to pursue our goals and redefine for myself instead what progress, meaningful work, and a business owner can look like.[2]

It can be scary to rip up the rulebook, whether it's the able-bodied rulebook, the capitalist rulebook, or the "charge what you're worth" rule book. Rulebooks can be comforting; if we're not following a rulebook, what *can* we base our financial decisions around? Carrington suggests beginning by getting clear on two details: How much you need to earn per year from the services you provide to feel financially sustainable, and how much availability you want to have each year for this service.[3]

Importantly, these two questions are not equations for earning more and more and more. Neither are they questions that ask us to assign a dollar value to our self-worth. Rather, they encourage us to think about how much income we truly need to support the life we choose, and then help us figure out how to fill that need. Sometimes financial success is not about more work or more money, but about reaching and sustaining a balance of work and income that allows us to maintain balance in the rest of our lives.

Compromising Our Financial Stability Is Not a Useful Path Toward Justice

Surveys indicate that cost remains the primary barrier for people seeking mental health services, particularly for those most in need of them. This fact underlies the increasing public advocacy and pressure to make psychological services affordable for the general public. The vast majority of professionals in the field have shown strong support for this goal. For example, a position statement made by the Psychologists' Association of Alberta says that "all Albertans, regardless of income, should have access to psychological services."[4]

We recognize that many people do not have private insurance benefits and must pay out of pocket to access our services. For those who do have insurance, they may only have coverage for a handful of sessions, after which they, too, must pay out of pocket. The public system, meanwhile, is overloaded and often limited to short-term interventions, which are not necessarily appropriate for Canadians dealing with complex needs. These facts disproportionately affect those who are financially marginalized and may not have room in their budgets to pay out of pocket, or to do so regularly. In Canada, then, we effectively have a two-tiered system where those who can financially afford timely and long-term psychological services receive it, and those who cannot do not. Yet those in the second category are also more likely to be experiencing other forms of marginalization, strains on their mental health, or psychological illness. The access issue deepens when burnt-out therapists leave the public system for private practice (a necessary decision many people make to protect their own wellness), further lowering the capacity of the public system.

As a therapist, the solution to these problems is not to go into financial hardship or continue burning out in a broken system. Kelly Diels, a Canadian writer and feminist business coach, reminds us that individually shouldering the responsibility of fixing systemic issues often serves to perpetuate the systems we are trying to fight: "What I see happening on the back-end is that entrepreneurs with deep social commitments start thinking the only way to do businesses is to drastically reduce prices—often way below the actual cost of doing business. They then have to get second jobs, work 18 hour days, or go deeply into debt in order to operate an 'accessible business'. That's not collective well-being or collective justice."[5] Likewise, therapists in the public system may be encouraged to accept lower-paying jobs in order to be of service to marginalized communities. But low prices and low wages are not always possible for one-to-one service providers, especially those who are relying on one income.

It may help to remember that what we're really aiming for is *economic justice*. Ebony Butler emphasizes this point from her perspective as a Black licensed psychologist:

> Black therapists deserve a life of ease. Period. They don't
> deserve to be stressed out about money because systems are
> failing and mental health is not prioritized. They do not owe
> society their own mental health because systems have failed
> people who look like them. Because they want to spend time
> with their families too. They want to go on vacations like

> everybody else. They want to live a life of quality just like they
> encourage their clients to create. They can't do that if they're
> constantly setting and accepting low rates.[6]

Butler's point focuses on the extra pressures many marginalized therapists face to overwork and underpay themselves, a topic we discussed in chapter 4. She shifts the broader conversation towards humanizing therapists by making space for them to have needs, too.

The whole point of social justice movements is to improve *everyone's* quality of life and ability to be free and thrive. "Accessibility" and "affordability" are ways to describe a desire to provide inclusive and equitable services, but if they don't apply to both the client and the service provider, they are not economically just. There are many reasons why therapy is expensive, from unpaid consulting and case-formulation hours to business operating costs. These costs are real and need to be appropriately compensated. As Diels puts it,

> If low prices don't cover the actual costs of the business,
> then they have to [be] offset by other sources of income like
> grants, 2nd jobs, partners, family or trust funds—which might
> not be options for most people (which is the definition of
> inaccessible).
>
> Downloading collective oppression onto the shoulders of one
> individual is not justice (nor is it sustainable).[7]

The cost-burden of counselling and psychological services shouldn't fall on individual clients any more than it should fall on individual therapists. It's important to realize, however, that there are many ways to contribute to economic justice beyond offering low prices that imperil our businesses or accepting low wages that threaten our ability to survive. One big way is advocacy. We must continue fighting for economic justice, for ourselves and our clients, on a broader scale.

Advocacy is another responsibility that is difficult to shoulder alone. Consider looking for advocacy groups in your area that are already involved in economic justice campaigns (or creating one with a group of like-minded peers!). One group in Alberta, the Expert Psychologists Interagency Clinical Network (EPIC), has been doing great work in this area, including campaigns petitioning the provincial government to fund interventions with a psychologist and to allow psychologists to direct-bill Alberta Health Services for psychological services.[8] From EPIC's perspective, this approach would take pressure off the public mental health system, which is currently not able to provide accessible, timely, or proactive interventions for psychological issues. You may also look at bigger organizations such as the American Psychological Association (APA) or Canadian

Psychological Association (CPA) to find out how you can get involved with their advocacy efforts.

There is more than one way to justly address issues of affordability and accessibility of mental health services. Provincial or federal governments could set aside money to specifically fund psychological services and offset costs. Insurance companies could cover more sessions per year so that the services covered align more with psychological need. We can't create these changes alone, but we can advocate for such changes while still practising sustainably.

Reflect and Journal

What are your current beliefs around money? Are there any old beliefs you've been operating by that you'd like to let go of? Any new ones you'd like to embrace, with sustainability in mind?

Direct-Pay Clients and Third-Party Billing

Career satisfaction among psychologists, compared to other professionals, tends to be quite high,[9] but certain factors are associated with the highest satisfaction. These include percentage of direct-pay clients, work–life balance strategies, control at work, and reflecting on satisfying work experiences.[10]

I want to highlight one of these factors in particular: direct-pay clients. As one study pointed out, when third-party payers are involved, there may be some disadvantages that result in an increased workload, such as extra paperwork. Having a lot of third-party payers may also mean losing control over treatment decisions (including the number of sessions allowed) and receiving less compensation. Direct-pay clients, by contrast, may allow for more flexibility and adaptability, with fewer external restrictions.[11]

Another study, focusing on public-sector workers in Malta, indicated that psychologists tended to perceive negative experiences in the public health system as more distressing than those arising from private client work. The study found, again, that a feeling of lack of control played a big part in this distress, as did feelings of powerlessness and divergent values, all of which appear to contribute to reduced job engagement.[12]

Know that you *can* work in the public system or in third-party-payer situations and be quite satisfied. If you are in these situations, though, you may need to be especially conscientious of how you approach your work environment. Intentionally making space to take in and acknowledge rewarding aspects of your work is especially important. This may include noticing and celebrating the improvements clients make over the course of therapy, feeling appreciated by clients, and attending to opportunities for and experiences of growth. It could also include finding a community of like-minded psychologists from whom you can access peer support.[13]

Protecting Your Financial Boundaries in Private Practice

Certain questions come up so often for therapists in private practice settings that they warrant some focused attention. I'll go over three of them here:

1. What is my cancellation/no-show policy?
2. How will I handle nonpayment?
3. What are my typical fees, and will I offer sliding scale / reduced-fee spots?

Cancellation / No-Show Policies

A common cancellation policy allows clients to cancel an appointment up to 24 to 48 hours before it is scheduled without incurring a cancellation fee. If clients cancel after this window, they are charged a fee, which might be equivalent to the fee of an attended session or a percentage of that fee. Some therapists choose to waive the cancellation fee under certain circumstances, while others have a stricter policy. Some therapists feel that a one-time fee forgiveness per client fits best. Whatever policy you decide to put in place, make sure you have one, make it clear, and are consistent in how you apply it. Basing our policies on how we feel about a particular client or our mood on a given day can create resentment in us and confusion in clients.

Any policy you develop in your practice should be rooted in your guiding values. If your policies don't reflect your values, you may find them especially difficult to apply. They may feel confusing or flat-out wrong to you, and this can, again, lead to inconsistency and resentment. While applying policies can itself be a difficult and sometimes uncomfortable practice for some therapists, it is an important aspect of keeping yourself safe and defining the boundaries of the therapeutic and financial relationship. Value-based policies get easier to sustainably apply over time.

A guiding value in my work is having the space and ability to listen to my body; I value this for my clients as well. Here's an example of a clear cancellation policy I developed that reflects this value:

> I understand that there will be times you will not be able to make your scheduled appointment. I kindly request 48 hours cancellation notice to avoid a cancellation fee of $110. If a

no-show occurs or cancellation with less than 24 hours' notice
is given, the full fee of the service will be charged. I will waive
the fee if notice is given and the reason for cancellation is pain
or illness.

Once you have a clear policy, you'll want to ask yourself how you plan
to enforce it. For example, some therapists require clients to provide a
credit card number in order book with them. This allows them to process
fees without delay, or to have a regular time when they complete client
transactions—for example, at the beginning of the day, or at the start of
each session, prior to services being provided. Others may have a policy that
a subsequent session cannot be booked until the previous session is paid for.

A colleague of mine takes a very straightforward approach. The kindness
is in the clear and judgment-free language. Here's her suggestion for handling cancellation fees:

Hi [client],

I noticed that you cancelled our appointment today. I've
attached the invoice for the late-cancellation fee. Please let me
know if there are extenuating circumstances I should be aware
of, and otherwise pay the balance within (48) hours of receiving this invoice.

As with any boundary, it's important to prepare yourself for the work of
practising and respecting your financial boundaries as reflections of your
needs, and for the fact that others may not be prepared to offer that same
respect. Know that you will likely have clients who will not respond posi-
tively to being asked to pay a no-show fee and may seek ways to avoid paying it. I have heard a variety of reasons from clients for why they don't want
to pay a cancellation fee, from not getting a reminder call to not being able
to afford it. Within the confines of a trusting relationship, these situations
can be good fodder for therapeutic work. However, if a client cannot abide
by the boundaries that sustain you, this may mean it's time to pause the
work. You can reinforce with clients that it is their responsibility to make it
to their scheduled appointment and pay any fees associated with it. You can
also offer other therapeutic options that are more flexible about the areas
that are non-negotiable for you.

Nonpayment

If clients have a consistently hard time with financial boundaries, you
can gently approach them about ways of adjusting your financial relationship that could support both of you. Here's one example of a template
email I send to clients who are having a hard time paying on time for
their appointments:

> Dear [client],
>
> Hope you're well. I'm just going over my financial records for the year and it looks like there's a balance on your file of [dollar amount] for an appointment on [date]. Is this something you'd be able to pay this week? I talked with a couple other clients at the end of the year and I understand that people sometimes get behind because they forget, and sometimes because they don't have the money at the exact time of the appointment. I now have the ability to put credit cards on file and I can run it through for you on the day of our appointment. Would this work for you? Please let me know.

I have found that when I approach the problem with curiosity about what might work better for us both, most clients are happy to work together to find a solution. In cases where your client is having trouble affording your full rate and you aren't in a position to offer a reduced rate, this type of discussion can be important and productive. In some cases, a discussion around nonpayment may involve suggesting other therapeutic options to your client.

Most therapists I have talked to have said that, as they got into the habit of sending invoices for unpaid sessions and following up on them, they became more comfortable applying their billing and nonpayment policies. Of course, everyone's comfort level is different, as is how they want to go about implementing their boundaries. You may choose to have an administrative staff handle finances if that helps you create a more comfortable distance. Ultimately, you must be comfortable enforcing the policies you develop; this is the only way they will be sustainable for you.

Fees and Sliding Scale

Many therapists, new ones especially, work on a volunteer basis or sliding scale without having a realistic look at how this will impact their income or their workload, or how many full-paying clients they need to sustain their work with reduced-fee clients. Many also struggle with having a fee that is consistent with the recommended rates. I certainly struggled with this for years, as I worried the recommended rate was too much for the clients I was seeing. In practice, this meant I had more clients on reduced rates than I could afford to keep there. At one point, a friend suggested I keep my reduced rates where they were but increase my upper-limit rates. Clients who already had insurance or the means to pay the full fee would likely not be as affected by a price increase as those who were accessing the reduced-fee spots, and I would be able to pay my bills.

Some therapists I've spoken to notice that they have a habit of offering clients pro bono services before they have considered if it is in their budget to do so, and before they have considered any other options. Remember that when a client mentions financial stress, this is only the start of a conversation. If you are able to take a pause, you may find there are options other than pro bono or even reduced-rate service that work well for both of you. For clients with limited means, this may include spacing out sessions but giving homework and reflection practices to complete between sessions. If the client needs to see someone more often, you might refer them to other therapists or organizations in your network who offer a reduced rate and whose work you trust. Beyond peer support, this is an important reason to develop a network of like-minded practitioners who you trust: We cannot be the only option we know of for our clients.

If you do plan to offer reduced fees, think carefully about how you will organize it. Some therapists have a set reduced rate they can offer to those who need it. Others have the client choose a fee within a broad range. Still others might use a client's income to decide their fee. In all cases, think about the number of clients you are able to see in a week and about the amount of income you need to sustain your practice and your life. Use this information to inform how many reduced-fee or pro bono clients you can realistically take on, and at what frequency.

Keep in mind, too, that what has worked for you before or what works for you now in terms of financial boundaries may not always work for you. For example, some therapists find that when they have few spots available, perhaps because they're handling parenting responsibilities or taking care of an aging parent at home, they are less able to offer reduced-fee spots. (They may find the opposite as their home responsibilities lessen and they can give more time to work.) You may also choose to raise your fees as the cost of living rises. Generally, most clients understand that fees change over the years, but it can help to provide ample notice of a fee change, and to offer clients an opportunity to discuss any concerns with you before the new fee is implemented.

Boundary Practice

If you're working in private practice or planning to, take the time now to draft your policies on fees and cancellations. What policies will help sustain your emotional and financial well-being, and your time boundaries?

If you work in the public sector, review your current employment benefits and explore opportunities for negotiation. This may include seeking additional benefits such as professional-development stipends, flexible work arrangements, or wellness programs.

Final Reflection

From start to finish, I designed this book to be an invitation to turn toward yourself and to remember the importance of preserving your humanity while helping others. Setting boundaries helps us not only avoid burnout, resentment, and vicarious trauma, but also increase satisfaction in our lives and work. Healing is an endeavour that we work on with others, but it must also include ourselves.

This is so foundational to our work as therapists. We do difficult, necessary, emotional work with our clients—work that, we hope, helps them to live full, abundant, fulfilling, and deeply human lives. I hope the same for you, too. Remember that you are a human first, a therapist after. Prioritizing this fact will help you to live a full, abundant life in which you remain connected to who you are and what makes you feel like yourself—and this, in turn, will help you connect more authentically, deeply, and easefully with others, in both your work and your private life.

By practising joy and ease in our lives, we expand the possibilities for all of us—our colleagues, our clients, our friends and family, our community, our world. By allowing ourselves to say no to what doesn't work, we can open ourselves up to what does. We are left with more energy, time, and life to give to what matters most to us, what we want to say yes to. We are left with more possibilities for joy, delight, awe, connection, meaning, and anything else that nurtures our humanity. Our work is a part of such a life, but it is not the whole thing. The ability to have boundaries around our work allows us to show up more fully in our lives in the ways we hope those we help will be able to show up in theirs.

At the beginning of this book, I made a commitment to offering

Reflect and Journal

- What does living a good life look like for you, in this season of your life?
- How are you already tending to your joy?
- Where are you already feeling satisfaction and contentment in your life?
- What does satisfaction feel like in your body?

you, the reader, a space to reflect on your values, your capacity, and your needs. I hoped that by tuning into yourself through a compassionate lens, you would find more clarity about what sustainable work realistically looks like for you right now. I hope, now, that you can begin to put that clarity into practice.

Reflect and Journal

As you reflect back on what you've read, notice what you're taking away most of all.

- What did you learn about yourself?
- What did you learn about what you need to set and sustain boundaries?
- What are you proud of, even if it's something small? (And yes, I really would like you to come up with something.)
- What have you learned that you would most like to share with others?

Notes

Introduction

1. C.M. Lee, E.D Reissing, and D. Dobson, "Work-Life Balance for Early Career Canadian Psychologists in Professional Programs," *Canadian Psychology / Psychologie canadienne* 50, no. 2 (2009): 74–82, https://doi.org/10.1037/a0013871; K.A. Maranzan, K.R. Kowatch, B.A. Mascioli, L. McGeown, A.D. Popowich, and F. Spiroiu, "Self-Care and the Canadian Code of Ethics: Implications for Training in Professional Psychology," *Canadian Psychology / Psychologie canadienne* 59, no. 4 (2018): 361–368, https://doi.org/10.1037/cap0000153.

2. M.G. Turnbull and P. Rhodes, "Burnout and Growth: Narratives of Australian Psychologists," *Qualitative Psychology* 8, no. 1 (2021): 51–61, https://doi.org/10.1037/qup0000146.

Chapter 1. Boundaries Make Room for Yes

1. Tricia Hersey (@TheNapMinistry), "You can really, really love the work you do," tweet, July 3, 2022, https://twitter.com/TheNapMinistry/status/1295378129956081664.

2. Lisa Olivera, "What I Want," *Human Stuff*, July 3, 2022, https://lisaolivera.substack.com/p/what-i-want.

3. Ariel Gore, *The Mother Trip: Hip Mamas Guide to Staying Sane in the Chaos of Motherhood* (Pymble, New South Wales: HarperCollins, 2000).

4. adrienne maree brown and Sonya Renee Taylor, *Journal of Radical Permission: A Daily Guide for Following Your Soul's Calling* (Oakland, CA: Berret-Koehler, 2022).

5. brown, "Dearest Liberator of the Self and the Collective," in brown and Taylor, *Journal of Radical Permission*, frontmatter.

6. Franklin Veaux and Eve Rickert, *More Than Two: A Practical Guide to Ethical Polyamory* (Portland, OR: Thorntree Press, 2014), 156.

7. Harriet Lerner, *The Dance of Anger: A Woman's Guide to Changing the Patterns of Intimate Relationships* (New York, NY: Avon Publications, 2005), 14.

8. Melody Li, "How to Set Culturally Attuned Boundaries and Why It Matters in Therapy," *Inclusivetherapists.com* (blog), February 21, 2020, https://www.inclusivetherapists.com/blog/how-to-set-culturally-attuned-boundaries-and-why-it-matters-in-therapy.

9. D. Wiens, J. Theule, J. Keates, M. Ward, and A. Yaholkoski. "Work–Family Balance and Job Satisfaction: An Analysis of Canadian Psychologist Mothers." *Canadian Psychology/Psychologie canadienne* 64, no. 2 (2023): 154–165, http://dx.doi.org/10.1037/cap0000321.

10. Lisa Olivera, "When Something No Longer Fits," *Human Stuff*, June 26, 2022, https://lisaolivera.substack.com/p/when-something-no-longer-fits.

11. Daniel J. Siegel, *The Developing Mind*, 3rd ed. (New York, NY: Guilford Press, 2020; originally published 1999).

12. I like to use the SCOPE tool from the Trauma Centre for this. See https://traumahealing.org/scope/.

13. Canadian Psychological Association, *Canadian Code of Ethics for Psychologists*, II.12; see also K.A. Maranzan et al., "Self-Care and the Canadian Code of Ethics."

14. D.E. Colman, R. Echon, M.S. Lemay, J. McDonald, K.R. Smith, J. Spencer, and J.K. Swift, "The Efficacy of Self-Care for Graduate Students in Professional Psychology: A Meta-Analysis," *Training and Education in Professional Psychology* 10, no. 4 (2016): 188–197, https://doi.org/10.1037/tep0000130.

15. Nakita Valerio quoted in Heather Dockray, "Self-Care Isn't Enough. We Need Community Care to Thrive," *Mashable*, May 24, 2019, https://mashable.com/article/community-care-versus-self-care.

16. E. Melaki and P.-D. Stavrou, "Re-exploring the Vicarious Posttraumatic Growth and Trauma: A Comparison Study Between Private Therapists and Therapists in Nonprofit Organizations Treating Trauma Survivors," *Traumatology* 29, no. 1 (2023), 27–35, https://doi.org/10.1037/trm0000378.

17. Turnbull and Rhodes, "Burnout and Growth."

Chapter 2. Boundaries Sustain Us

1. P.M. Bamonti, C.M. Keelan, N. Larson, J.M. Mentrikoski, C.L. Randall, S.K Sly, R.M. Travers, and D.W. McNeil, "Promoting Ethical Behavior by Cultivating a Culture of Self-Care During Graduate Training: A Call to Action," *Training and Education in Professional Psychology* 8, no. 4 (2014): 253–260, https://doi.org/10.1037/tep0000056.

2. Anne Helen Petersen, "How Millennials Became the Burnout Generation," *BuzzFeed*, January 5, 2019, https://www.buzzfeednews.com/article/annehelenpetersen/millennials-burnout-generation-debt-work.

3. O. Laverdière, D. Kealy, J.S. Ogrodniczuk, and A.J.S. Morin, "Psychological Health Profiles of Canadian Psychotherapists: A Wake Up Call on Psychotherapists' Mental Health," *Canadian Psychology / Psychologie canadienne* 59, no. 4 (2018): 315–322, https://doi.org/10.1037/cap0000159.

4. Turnbull and Rhodes, "Burnout and Growth."

5. Christina Maslach, *Burnout: The Cost of Caring* (Los Altos, CA: Institute for the Study of Human Knowledge, 2003).

6. Harvard Health Publishing, "Understanding the Stress Response" *Harvard Health Blog*, July 6, 2020, https://www.health.harvard.edu/staying-healthy/understanding-the-stress-response.

7. The American Institute of Stress, "Stress Effects," *The American Institute of Stress: Facts*, October 6, 2011, https://www.stress.org/stress-effects.

8. Harvard Medical Publishing, "Understanding the Stress Response."

9. Tiana Clark, "This Is What Black Burnout Feels Like," *BuzzFeed News*, January 11, 2019, https://www.buzzfeednews.com/article/tianaclarkpoet/millennial-burnout-black-women-self-care-anxiety-depression.

10. Sarah Deweerdt, "Autistic Burnout Explained," *Spectrum*, March 30, 2020, https://www.spectrumnews.org/news/autistic-burnout-explained/.

11. Jill Dahl, "Warning: 'Hanging In There' Is Destroying Your Health," *Daily Hive*, December 19, 2017, https://dailyhive.com/vancouver/warning-hanging-in-there-destroying-your-health.

12. Sherrie Bourg Carter, "The Tell Tale Signs Of Burnout ... Do You Have Them?" *Psychology Today*, November 26, 2013, https://www.psychologytoday.com/us/blog/high-octane-women/201311/the-tell-tale-signs-of-burnout-do-you-have-them.

13. Turnbull and Rhodes, "Burnout and Growth."

14. Turnbull and Rhodes, "Burnout and Growth"; P.A. Rupert, A.O. Miller, E.R. Tuminello Hartman, and F.B. Bryant, "Predictors of Career Satisfaction among Practicing Psychologists, *Professional Psychology: Research and Practice* 43, no. 5 (2012): 495–502, https://doi.org/10.1037/a0029420.

15. Maslach, *Burnout*, xxiii.

16. S.L. Mailloux, "The Ethical Imperative: Special Considerations in the Trauma Counseling Process," *Traumatology: An International Journal* 20, no. 1 (2014): 50–56, https://doi.org/10.1177/1534765613496649.

17. Nicole Perry, *Vicarious Trauma and Burnout: Inclusive Practices Guidelines for Assisting Newcomers to Canada* (Edmonton, AB: United Cultures of Canada, 2020), 5–6.

18. Mark Banschick, "Somatic Experiencing: How Trauma Can Be Overcome," *Psychology Today*, March 26, 2015, https://www.psychologytoday.com/ca/blog/the-intelligent-divorce/201503/somatic-experiencing.

19. National Institute for the Clinical Application of Behavioral Medicine, "4 Signs of the Attach/Cry-for-Help Response," *NICABM Blog*, accessed September 5, 2023, https://www.nicabm.com/identify-attach-cry-for-help/; National Institute for the Clinical Application of Behavioral medicine, "How to Differentiate between the Freeze and Shutdown Trauma Responses," *NICABM Blog*, accessed September 5, 2023, https://www.nicabm.com/the-difference-between-freeze-and-shutdown-trauma-responses/; Ron Siegel, "When the Fear of Rejection Leads to Appeasing Patterns," posted July 6, 2021, YouTube Video, 2:27, https://www.youtube.com/watch?v=nUqSkUkX_q4. See also the NICABM's advanced master's program How to Work with Emerging Defense Responses to Trauma (Beyond the Fight/Flight/Freeze Model), https://www.nicabm.com/program/beyond-fff/.

20. Françoise Mathieu, *The Compassion Fatigue Workbook: Creative Tools for Transforming Compassion Fatigue and Vicarious Traumatization* (Abingdon, UK: Taylor & Francis, 2012), 9.

21. Melaki and Stavrou, "Re-exploring the Vicarious Posttraumatic Growth and Trauma."

22. Mailloux, "The Ethical Imperative"; Lucy Sutton, Sarah Rowe, George Hammerton, and Jo Billings, "The Contribution of Organisational Factors to Vicarious Trauma in Mental Health Professionals: A Systematic Review and Narrative Synthesis," *European Journal of Psychotraumatology* 13, no. 1 (2022), https://doi.org/10.1080/20008198.2021.2022278; Ana B Méndez-Fernández, Francisco J. Aguiar-Fernández, Xoan Lombardero-Posada, Evelia Murcia-Álvarez, and Antonio González-Fernández, "Vicariously Resilient or Traumatised Social Workers: Exploring Some Risk and Protective Factors," *The British Journal of Social Work* 52, no. 2 (March 2022): 1089–1109, https://doi.org/10.1093/bjsw/bcab085.

23. Jude Mary Cénat, "Complex Racial Trauma: Evidence, Theory, Assessment, and Treatment," *Perspectives on Psychological Science* 18, no. 3 (2023): 675–687, https://doi.org/10.1177/17456916221120428.

24. *Oxford Languages*, Google ed., s.v. "resentment," https://www.google.com/search?client=firefox-b-d&q=definition+of+resentment.

25. brown and Taylor, *Journal of Radical Permission*, 15.

26. Nedra Tawwab (@nedratawwab), "You don't have to win the award for pain endurance," Instagram post, November 1, 2022, https://www.instagram.com/p/CkbUsJPueJ3/.

Chapter 3. Boundaries as Embodied Decisions

1. Jordan Pickell (@jordanpickellcounselling), "Some of us navigate relationships," Instagram post, February 24, 2021, https://www.instagram.com/p/CLs4h3UDeoc/.

2. Sonya Renee Taylor, *The Body Is Not an Apology: The Power of Radical Self-Love*, 2nd ed. (Oakland, CA: Berrett-Koehler Publishers, 2018), 50.

3. Strayed in Cheryl Strayed and Steve Almond, "Dear Sugar: How Do I Find the Courage to Be My Own Guide?" September 23, 2016, in *Dear Sugars*, produced by WBUR, podcast, 26:46, https://www.wbur.org/dearsugar/2016/09/23/dear-sugar-episode-seventy-one.

4. India Arie, interviewee, in Strayed and Almond, "Dear Sugar: How Do I Find the Courage."

Chapter 4. Barriers to Boundaries

1. Hoda Zahedi, Shirin Djalalinia, Omid Sadeghi, Fateme Zare Garizi, Hamid Asayesh, Moloud Payab, Maryam Zarei, and Mostafa Qorbani, "Breakfast Consumption and Mental Health: A Systematic Review and Meta-Analysis of Observational Studies," *Nutritional Neuroscience* 25, no. 6 (2020): 1250-1264, https://doi.org/10.1080/1028415X.2020.1853411.

2. Shuang Rong, Linda G. Snetselaar, Guifeng Xu, Yangbo Sun, Buyun Liu, Robert B. Wallace, and Wei Bao, "Association of Skipping Breakfast With Cardiovascular and All-Cause Mortality," Journal of the American College of Cardiology 73, no. 16 (April 2019): 2025–2032, https://doi.org/10.1016/j.jacc.2019.01.065.

3. Geisinger, "Stop Holding It In! 4 Bodily Functions You Should Let Out", *Balance by Geisinger*, March 29, 2018, https://www.geisinger.org/health-and-wellness/wellness-articles/2018/03/29/21/13/stop-holding-it-in-4-bodily-functions-you-should-let-out.

4. Leonie Kirszenblat, "Why Our Brain Needs Sleep, and What Happens If We Don't Get Enough of It," *The Conversation*, October 18, 2017, https://theconversation.com/why-our-brain-needs-sleep-and-what-happens-if-we-dont-get-enough-of-it-83145.

5. Jane E. Ferrie, Martin J. Shipley, Francesco P. Cappuccio, Eric Brunner, Michelle A. Miller, Meena Kumari, and Michael G. Marmot, "A Prospective Study of Change in Sleep Duration: Associations with Mortality in the Whitehall II Cohort," *Sleep* 30, no. 12 (2007): 1659-1666, https://doi.org/10.1093/sleep/30.12.1659.

6. Annina Seiler, Christopher P. Fagundes, and L.M. Christian, Lisa M., "The Impact of Everyday Stressors on the Immune System and Health," in *Stress Challenges and Immunity in Space*, ed. Alexander Choukèr (Berlin: Springer, 2020), 71–92, https://doi.org/10.1007/978-3-030-16996-1_6.

7. Ono Mergen (Onoceans), "You Don't Need to be Productive and Useful All of the Time," *Medium*, April 19, 2021, https://medium.com/swlh/you-dont-need-to-be-productive-and-useful-all-of-the-time-3e295cf19106.

8. Omid Safi, "The Disease Of Being Busy," *On Being*, November 6, 2014, https://onbeing.org/blog/the-disease-of-being-busy.

9. Ram Dass and Paul Gorman, *How Can I Help? Stories And Reflections On Service* (New York: Alfred A. Knopf, Inc., 2005).

10. Anne Helen Petersen, *Can't Even: How Millennials Became the Burnout Generation* (New York, NY: Houghton Mifflin Harcourt, 2021), 50.

11. Gabor Maté, *When the Body Says No: The Cost of Hidden Stress*, (Toronto: Vintage Canada, 2014), 224.

12. "Types of Leaves You Can Receive as an Employee Working in Federally Regulated Industries and Workplaces," Government of Canada, last modified October 6, 2023, https://www.canada.ca/en/employment-social-development/services/labour-standards/reports/bereavement-leave.html.

13. Emily Nagoski and Amelia Nagoski, *Burnout: The Secret to Unlocking the Stress Cycle* (New York, NY: Ballantine Books, 2019), 102.

14. Maté, *When the Body Says No*, 8.

15. Emily Field, Alexis Krivkovich, Sandra Kügele, Nicole Robinson, and Lareina Yee, *Women in the Workplace 2023* (n.p.: McKinsey & Company, 2023), https://www.mckinsey.com/featured-insights/diversity-and-inclusion/women-in-the-workplace-archive#section-header-2022.

16. Field et al., *Women in the Workplace 2023*.

17. Alberta Human Rights Act, RSA 2000, c A-25.5, 7(1).

18. "Discrimination," Alberta Human Rights Commission, accessed December 12, 2023, https://albertahumanrights.ab.ca/what-are-human-rights/about-human-rights/discrimination/.

19. "What Is the Duty to Accommodate," Canadian Human Rights Commission, accessed December 12, 2023, https://www.chrc-ccdp.gc.ca/en/about-human-rights/what-the-duty-accommodate.

20. Definition adapted from *Oxford Dictionaries Premium*, s.v. "emotional labour (*n.*)," accessed April 17, 2023, https://premium.oxforddictionaries.com/definition/english/emotional-labour.

21. Sheryl Nance-Nash, "How Corporate Diversity Initiatives Trap Workers of Colour," *BBC*, September 13, 2020, https://www.bbc.com/worklife/article/20200826-how-corporate-diversity-initiatives-trap-workers-of-colour; John Dujay, "How To Avoid 'Cultural Tax' of DEI Initiatives," *Canadian HR Reporter*, October 4, 2023, https://www.hrreporter.com/focus-areas/diversity/how-to-avoid-cultural-tax-of-dei-initiatives/380238.

22. Sinha, "Alleviating the Burden."

23. U. Hess, S. David, and S. Hareli, "Emotional Restraint Is Good for Men Only: The Influence of Emotional Restraint on Perceptions of Competence," *Emotion* 16, no. 2 (2016): 208–213, https://doi.org/10.1037/emo0000125.

24. Kai Cheng Thom, "8 Lessons That Show How Emotional Labor Defines Women's Lives," *Everyday Feminism*, June 15, 2016, http://everydayfeminism.com/2016/06/emotional-labor-womens-lives/.

25. L.G. Robertson, T.L. Anderson, M.E.L. Hall, and C.L. Kim, "Mothers and Mental Labor: A Phenomenological Focus Group Study of Family-Related Thinking Work," *Psychology of Women Quarterly* 43, no. 2 (2019): 184–200, https://doi.org/10.1177/0361684319825581; L. Ciciolla and S.S. Luthar, "Invisible Household Labor and Ramifications for Adjustment: Mothers as Captains of Households," *Sex Roles* 81 (2019): 467–486, https://doi.org/10.1007/s11199-018-1001-x; A. Hjálmsdóttir and V.S. Bjarnadóttir, "'I Have Turned into a Foreman Here at Home': Families and Work–Life Balance in Times of COVID-19 in a Gender Equality Paradise," *Gender Work Organ* 28 (2021): 268–283, https://doi.org/10.1111/gwao.12552.

26. Wiens et al., "Work–Family Balance and Job Satisfaction."

27. Wiens et al., "Work–Family Balance and Job Satisfaction," 159.

28. Judy Chu in Jennifer Siebel Newsom, dir., *The Mask You Live In* (n.p.: The Representation Project, 2015), digital streaming, 1:37:00.

29. Petersen, *Can't Even*, 50.

30. Oliver Burkeman, "This Column Will Change Your Life: The Protestant Work Ethic," *Guardian*, September 10, 2010, https://www.theguardian.com/lifeandstyle/2010/sep/11/pain-gain-work-ethic-burkeman.

31. Daniel Markovits, "How Meritocracy Harms Everyone—Even the Winners," interview by Sean Illing, *Vox*, December 14, 2019, https://www.vox.com/identities/2019/10/21/20897021/meritocracy-economic-mobility-daniel-markovits.

32. Petersen, *Can't Even*, xxii.

33. Sage Grayson, "The Not-to-Do List," accessed September 5, 2023, https://sagegrayson.com/wp-content/uploads/2014/03/Sage-Grayson-Not-To-Do-List.pdf.

34. Jordan Pickell (@jordanpickellcounselling), "When it comes to boundary setting," Instagram post, November 7, 2021, https://www.instagram.com/p/CV-qOvoJP3T/.

Chapter 5. Coping with Guilt and Shame

1. Harriet Lerner, *The Dance of Intimacy* (New York: HarperCollins, 2003), 67.

2. Lerner, *The Dance of Intimacy*, 67.

3. Brené Brown, "Listening to Shame," recorded March 12, 2012, TED talk, 14:38, https://brenebrown.com/videos/ted-talk-listening-to-shame/.

4. Brown, "Listening to Shame," 13:50–14:16.

5. Bret Lyon and Sheila Rubin, "Advanced 1: Giving Back the Shame," course presented through the Center for Healing Shame, online, October 9, 2020.

6. Bret Lyon and Sheila Rubin, *Embracing Shame: How to Stop Resisting Shame and Turn It into a Powerful Ally* (Boulder, CO: Sounds True, 2023).

7. The guilt trap is adapted from the original guilt wheel, created by Jen Thomson. Thank you Jen – it has been invaluable to my work.

8. Holly Martinez, "What Is Social Empowerment? Empowerment Definition and Theory," *United Way Blog*, May 24, 2022, https://unitedwaynca.org/blog/social-empowerment/.

9. Nedra Tawwab (@nedratawwab), "Sometimes trying to control the outcome," Instagram post, January 12, 2023, https://www.instagram.com/p/CnU7V3ZOYV8/.

10. Maté, *When the Body Says No*, 257.

11. Brené Brown, "Boundaries Featuring Brené Brown," accessed June 20, 2019, *The Work of the People*, video, 5:53, https://www.theworkofthepeople.com/boundaries.

12. Brown, "Boundaries Featuring Brené Brown."

13. Taylor, *The Body Is Not an Apology*, 13.

Chapter 6. Boundaries Around Our Emotions

1. L. Stelte and D. de Rosenroll, "Somatic Experiencing Intermediate I," course presented by Somatic Experiencing International, Edmonton, AB, May 6–9, 2016.

2. T. Eyal, M. Steffel, and N. Epley, "Perspective Mistaking: Accurately Understanding the Mind of Another Requires Getting Perspective, Not Taking Perspective," *Journal of Personality and Social Psychology* 114, no. 4 (2018): 547–571, https://doi.org/10.1037/pspa0000115; Anneke E.K. Bufonne, Michael Poulin, Shane DeLury, Lauren Ministero, Carrie Morrison, and Matt Scalco, "Don't Walk in Her Shoes! Different Forms of Perspective Taking Affect Stress Physiology," *Journal of Experimental Social Psychology* 72 (September 2017): 161–168, https://doi.org/10.1016/j.jesp.2017.04.001.

3. Eyal, Steffel, and Epley, "Perspective Mistaking."

4. Eyal, Steffel, and Epley, "Perspective Mistaking"; Anneke E.K. Buffone, Michalel Poulin, Shane DeLury, Lauren Ministero, Carrie Morrisson, and Matt Scalco, "Don't Walk in Her Shoes! Different Forms of Perspective Taking Affect Stress Physiology," *Journal of Experimental Social Psychology* 72 (September 2017): 161–168, https://doi.org/10.1016/j.jesp.2017.04.001.

5. Stelte and de Rosenroll, "Somatic Experiencing Intermediate I."

6. Nicole Perry, *Intimate Partner Violence: Inclusive Practices Guidelines for Assisting Newcomers to Canada* (Edmonton, AB: United Cultures of Canada, 2020), p. 76.

7. L. Stelte and B. Galloway, "Somatic Experiencing Beginning III," course presented by Somatic Experiencing International, Edmonton, AB, January 22–25, 2016.

8. Meg Berryman, "Why am I STILL burnt out?" newsletter, September 13, 2022, https://www.megberryman.com/.

9. Turnbull and Rhodes, "Burnout and Growth."

10. Turnbull and Rhodes, "Burnout and Growth."

11. S. Michalchuk and S.L. Martin, "Vicarious Resilience and Growth in Psychologists Who Work with Trauma Survivors: An Interpretive Phenomenological Analysis," *Professional Psychology: Research and Practice* 50, no. 3 (2019): 145–154, https://doi.org/10.1037/pro0000212.

Chapter 7. Boundaries Around Our Time and Attention

1. P.A. Rupert, E.R.T. Hartman, and A.S.O. Miller, "Work Demands and Resources, Work–Family Conflict, and Family Functioning among Practicing Psychologists," *Professional Psychology: Research and Practice* 44, no. 5 (2019): 283–289, https://doi.org/10.1037/a0034494; K. Posluns and T.L. Gall, "Dear Mental Health Practitioners, Take Care of Yourselves: A Literature Review on Self-Care," *International Journal for the Advancement of Counseling* 42, no. 1 (2019): 1–20, https://doi.org/10.1007/s10447-019-09382-w.

2. Johann Hari, *Stolen Focus: Why You Can't Pay Attention—and How to Think Deeply Again* (New York: Crown, 2021).

3. Perry, *Vicarious Trauma & Burnout*.

4. Wiens et al., "Work–Family Balance and Job Satisfaction."

5. Jasmin Akbari, "Opinion: Combatting Toxic Academic Culture—Work to Learn, Not Work to Work," *The Varsity*, March 14, 2021, https://thevarsity.ca/2021/03/14/opinion-combatting-toxic-academic-culture-work-to-learn-not-work-to-work/; Christine Liu, "Imposter Syndrome Isn't the Problem—Toxic Workplaces Are," *Quartz*, May 23, 2018, https://qz.com/work/1286549/imposter-syndrome-lets-toxic-work-culture-off-the-hook.

6. Melaki and Stavrou, "Re-exploring the Vicarious Posttraumatic Growth and Trauma."

7. Perry, *Vicarious Trauma & Burnout*.

Chapter 8. Boundaries Around Our Workplaces and Finances

1. Meg Selig, "9 Surprising Superpowers of Knowing Your Core Values," *Psychology Today*, November 27, 2018, https://www.psychologytoday.com/ca/blog/changepower/201811/9-surprising-superpowers-knowing-your-core-values.

2. Jen Carrington, email newsletter, August 30, 2021.

3. Jen Carrington, email newsletter, March 1, 2021.

4. "About PAA," Psychologists' Association of Alberta, accessed June 10, 2023, https://psychologistsassociation.ab.ca/about/.

5. Kelly Diels (@kelly.diels), "Right now, there's a lot of conversation pushing back on what's perceived as higher prices," Instagram post, October 4, 2022, https://www.instagram.com/p/CjTE2fKu_k_/.

6. Ebony Butler (@drebonyonline), "Today is Black Women's Equal Pay Day," Instagram post, September 21, 2022, https://www.instagram.com/p/CiyZfZ1r5bx/.

7. Diels, "Right now."

8. See, for example, EPIC's Change.org petition: https://www.change.org/p/petition-to-provide-provincially-funded-psychological-services-in-alberta.

9. Rupert et al., "Predictors of Career Satisfaction."

10. Rupert et al., "Predictors of Career Satisfaction."

11. Rupert et al., "Predictors of Career Satisfaction."

12. A. Sciberras and L. Pilkington, "The Lived Experience of Psychologists Working in Mental Health Services: An Exhausting and Exasperating Journey," *Professional Psychology: Research and Practice* 49, no. 2 (2018): 151–158, https://doi.org/10.1037/pro0000184.

13. Rupert et al., "Predictors of Career Satisfaction."

About the Author

Nicole Perry is a registered psychologist with a general private practice in Edmonton. She specializes in shame resilience, healing trauma, and setting boundaries. In her work as a psychologist today, Nicole uses a mix of somatic experiencing, a body-based therapy for healing trauma, and somatic- and attachment-focused EMDR. She also uses imaginal and mindful approaches to help clients heal painful wounds from the past. Nicole approaches her healing work with warmth and curiosity, and offers people a safe container for working with difficult experiences. She also helps people who are struggling with burnout and learning to say no.

Perry holds a master's degree in counselling psychology from Yorkville University and an undergraduate degree in psychology with a minor in creative writing from the University of Alberta. She maintains a blog (embodiedpsychology.ca) where she regularly discusses mental health issues from a feminist lens.